Reading STREET

Grade 2

Scott Foresman

Leveled Reader

Teaching Guide

D1466543

PEARSON

Scott Foresman

Editorial Offices: Glenview, Illinois • Parsippany, New Jersey • New York, New York
Sales Offices: Boston, Massachusetts • Duluth, Georgia • Glenview, Illinois
Coppell, Texas • Sacramento, California • Mesa, Arizona

ISBN: 0-328-16908-0

5 6 7 8 9 10 V084 12 11 10 09 08 07

Table of Contents

LEVELED READER TITLE	Instruction	Comprehension Practice	Vocabulary Practice
City Mouse and Country Mouse	12–13	14	15
Being an Astronaut	16–17	18	19
Pup Camps Out	20–21	22	23
Desert	24–25	26	27
The Case of the Missing Fish	28–29	30	31
Dogs to the Rescue	32–33	34	35
Let's Play Baseball!	36–37	38	39
Busy Beavers	40–41	42	43
Dogs at Work	44–45	46	47
Together for Thanksgiving	48–49	50	51
The Science Fair	52–53	54	55
How Does the Mail Work?	56–57	58	59
Casting Nets	60–61	62	63
Shy Ana	64–65	66	67
An Orange Floats	68–69	70	71
The Butterfly Quilt	72–73	74	75
Grow a Tomato!	76–77	78	79
A Frog's Life	80–81	82	83

© Pearson Education

Graphic Organizers

Introduction

Scott Foresman *Reading Street* provides over 600 leveled readers that help children become better readers and build a lifelong love of reading. The *Reading Street* leveled readers are engaging texts that help children practice critical reading skills and strategies. They also provide opportunities to build vocabulary, understand concepts, and develop reading fluency.

The leveled readers were developed to be age-appropriate and appealing to children at each grade level. The leveled readers consist of engaging texts in a variety of genres, including fantasy, folk tales, realistic fiction, historical fiction, and narrative and expository nonfiction. To better address real-life reading skills that children will encounter in testing situations and beyond, a higher percentage of nonfiction texts is provided at each grade.

USING THE LEVELED READERS

You can use the leveled readers to meet the diverse needs of your children. Consider using the readers to

- practice critical skills and strategies
- build fluency
- build vocabulary and concepts
- build background for the main selections in the student book
- provide a variety of reading experiences, e.g., shared, group, individual, take-home, readers' theater

GUIDED READING APPROACH

The *Reading Street* leveled readers are leveled according to Guided Reading criteria by experts trained in Guided Reading. The Guided Reading levels increase in difficulty within a grade level and across grade levels. In addition to leveling according to Guided Reading criteria, the instruction provided in the *Leveled Reader Teaching Guide* is compatible with Guided Reading instruction. An instructional routine is provided for each leveled reader. This routine is most effective when working with individual children or small groups.

MANAGING THE CLASSROOM

When using the leveled readers with individuals or small groups, you'll want to keep the other children engaged in meaningful, independent learning tasks. Establishing independent work stations throughout the classroom and child routines for these work stations can help you manage the rest of the class while you work with individuals or small groups. Possible work stations include Listening, Phonics, Vocabulary, Independent Reading, and Cross-Curricular. For classroom management, create a work board that lists the work stations and which children should be at each station. Provide instructions at each station that detail the tasks to be accomplished. Update the board and alert children when they should rotate to a new station. For additional support for managing your classroom, see the *Reading Street Centers Survival Kit.*

USING THE LEVELED READER TEACHING GUIDE

The *Leveled Reader Teaching Guide* provides an instruction plan for each leveled reader based on the same instructional routine.

INTRODUCE THE BOOK The Introduction includes suggestions for creating interest in the text by discussing the title and author, building background, and previewing the book and its features.

READ THE BOOK Before children begin reading the book, have them set purposes for reading and discuss how they can use the reading strategy as they read. Determine how you want children in a particular group to read the text, softly or silently, to a specific point or the entire text. Then use the Comprehension Questions to provide support as needed and to assess comprehension.

REVISIT THE BOOK The Think and Share questions provide opportunities for children to demonstrate their understanding of the text, the target comprehension skill, and vocabulary. The Response Options require children to revisit the text to respond to what they've read and to move beyond the text to explore related content.

SKILL WORK The Skill Work box provides instruction and practice for the target skill and strategy and selection vocabulary. Instruction for an alternate comprehension skill allows teachers to provide additional skill instruction and practice for children.

USING THE GRAPHIC ORGANIZERS

Graphic organizers in blackline-master format can be found on pages 132–152. These can be used as overhead transparencies or as worksheets.

ASSESSING PERFORMANCE

Use the assessment forms that begin on page 6 to make notes about your children's reading skills, use of reading strategies, and general reading behaviors.

MEASURE FLUENT READING (pp. 6–7) Provides directions for measuring a child's fluency, based on words correct per minute (wcpm), and reading accuracy using a running record.

OBSERVATION CHECKLIST (p. 8) Allows you to note the regularity with which children demonstrate their understanding and use of reading skills and strategies.

READING BEHAVIORS CHECKLIST (p. 9) Provides criteria for monitoring certain reading behaviors.

READING STRATEGY ASSESSMENT (p. 10) Provides criteria for evaluating each child's proficiency as a strategic reader.

PROGRESS REPORT (p. 11) Provides a means to track a child's book-reading progress over a period of time by noting the level at which a child reads and his or her accuracy at that level. Reading the chart from left to right gives you a visual model of how quickly a child is making the transition from one level to the next. Share these reports with parents or guardians to help them see how their child's reading is progressing.

Measure
Fluent Reading

Taking a Running Record

A running record is an assessment of a child's oral reading accuracy and oral reading fluency. Reading accuracy is based on the number of words read correctly. Reading fluency is based on the reading rate (the number of words correct per minute) and the degree to which a child reads with a "natural flow."

How to Measure Reading Accuracy

1. Choose a grade-level text of about 80 to 120 words that is unfamiliar to the child.
2. Make a copy of the text for yourself. Make a copy for the child or have the child read aloud from a book.
3. Give the child the text and have the child read aloud. (You may wish to record the child's reading for later evaluation.)
4. On your copy of the text, mark any miscues or errors the child makes while reading. See the running record sample on page 7, which shows how to identify and mark miscues.
5. Count the total number of words in the text and the total number of errors made by the child. Note: If a child makes the same error more than once, such as mispronouncing the same word multiple times, count it as one error. Self-corrections do not count as actual errors. Use the following formula to calculate the percentage score, or accuracy rate:

$$\frac{\text{Total Number of Words} - \text{Total Number of Errors}}{\text{Total Number of Words}} \times 100 = \text{percentage score}$$

Interpreting the Results

- A child who reads **95–100%** of the words correctly is reading at an **independent level** and may need more challenging text.
- A child who reads **90–94%** of the words correctly is reading at an **instructional level** and will likely benefit from guided instruction.
- A child who reads **89%** or fewer of the words correctly is reading at a **frustrational level** and may benefit most from targeted instruction with lower-level texts and intervention.

How to Measure Reading Rate (WCPM)

1. Follow Steps 1–3 above.
2. Note the exact times when the child begins and finishes reading.
3. Use the following formula to calculate the number of words correct per minute (WCPM):

$$\frac{\text{Total Number of Words Read Correctly}}{\text{Total Number of Seconds}} \times 60 = \text{words correct per minute}$$

Interpreting the Results

By the end of the year, a second-grader should be reading approximately 90–100 WCPM.

Running Record Sample

Running Record Sample

Running Record Sample

Just then a fly crawled near Fred.
Fred's long, sticky tongue shot out in a
flash and caught the tiny insect.
    "Delicious! I'm full now," he said
loudly. He had already eaten three other
insects and a worm in the past hour.
    Frankie overheard Fred and climbed
down a few branches. He moved
quickly and easily without falling.
    "What are you doing, Fred?" he
asked in a friendly voice.
    "I was just finishing up my lunch,"
Fred answered. "How is life up high
today, my friend?"

—From *Frog Friends*
On-Level Reader 2.4.3

Notations

Accurate Reading
The child reads a word correctly.

Insertion
The child inserts words or parts of words that are not in the text.

Mispronunciation/Misreading
The child pronounces or reads a word incorrectly.

Hesitation
The child hesitates over a word, and the teacher provides the word. Wait several seconds before telling the child what the word is.

Self-correction
The child reads a word incorrectly but then corrects the error. Do not count self-corrections as actual errors. However, noting self-corrections will help you identify words the child finds difficult.

Omission
The child omits words or word parts.

Substitution
The child substitutes words or parts of words for the words in the text.

Running Record Results
Total Number of Words: **86**
Number of Errors: **5**

Reading Time: **64 seconds**

▶ **Reading Accuracy**
$\frac{86 - 5}{86} \times 100 = 94.186 = 94\%$

Accuracy Percentage Score: **94%**

▶ **Reading Rate—WCPM**
$\frac{81}{64} \times 60 = 75.9 = 76$ words correct per minute

Reading Rate: **76 WCPM**

Observation Checklist

Child's Name _____ Date _____

Behaviors Observed	Always (Proficient)	Usually (Fluent)	Sometimes (Developing)	Rarely (Novice)
Reading Strategies and Skills				
Uses prior knowledge and preview to understand what book is about				
Makes predictions and checks them while reading				
Uses context clues to figure out meanings of new words				
Uses phonics and syllabication to decode words				
Self-corrects while reading				
Reads at an appropriate reading rate				
Reads with appropriate intonation and stress				
Uses fix-up strategies				
Identifies story elements: character, setting, plot, theme				
Summarizes plot or main ideas accurately				
Uses target comprehension skill to understand the text better				
Responds thoughtfully about the text				

Reading Behaviors and Attitudes

Enjoys listening to stories				
Chooses reading as a free-time activity				
Reads with sustained interest and attention				
Participates in discussion about books				

General Comments

Reading Behaviors Checklist

Child's Name _____   Date _____

Behavior	Yes	No	Not Applicable
Recognizes letters of the alphabet			
Recognizes name in print			
Recognizes some environmental print, such as signs and logos			
Knows the difference between letters and words			
Knows the difference between capital and lowercase letters			
Understands function of capitalization and punctuation			
Recognizes that book parts, such as the cover, title page, and table of contents, offer information			
Recognizes that words are represented in writing by specific sequences of letters			
Recognizes words that rhyme			
Distinguishes rhyming and nonrhyming words			
Knows letter-sound correspondences			
Identifies and isolates initial sounds in words			
Identifies and isolates final sounds in words			
Blends sounds to make spoken words			
Segments one-syllable spoken words into individual phonemes			
Reads consonant blends and digraphs			
Reads and understands endings, such as *-es, -ed, -ing*			
Reads vowels and vowel diphthongs			
Reads and understands possessives			
Reads and understands compound words			
Reads simple sentences			
Reads simple stories			
Understands simple story structure			
Other:			

Reading Strategy Assessment

Child _____ Date _____

Teacher _____

		Proficient	Developing	Emerging	Not showing trait
Building Background Comments:	Previews	☐	☐	☐	☐
	Asks questions	☐	☐	☐	☐
	Predicts	☐	☐	☐	☐
	Activates prior knowledge	☐	☐	☐	☐
	Sets own purposes for reading	☐	☐	☐	☐
	Other:	☐	☐	☐	☐
Comprehension Comments:	Retells/summarizes	☐	☐	☐	☐
	Questions, evaluates ideas	☐	☐	☐	☐
	Relates to self/other texts	☐	☐	☐	☐
	Paraphrases	☐	☐	☐	☐
	Rereads/reads ahead for meaning	☐	☐	☐	☐
	Visualizes	☐	☐	☐	☐
	Uses decoding strategies	☐	☐	☐	☐
	Uses vocabulary strategies	☐	☐	☐	☐
	Understands key ideas of a text	☐	☐	☐	☐
	Other:	☐	☐	☐	☐
Fluency Comments:	Adjusts reading rate	☐	☐	☐	☐
	Reads for accuracy	☐	☐	☐	☐
	Uses expression	☐	☐	☐	☐
	Other:	☐	☐	☐	☐
Connections Comments:	Relates text to self	☐	☐	☐	☐
	Relates text to text	☐	☐	☐	☐
	Relates text to world	☐	☐	☐	☐
	Other:	☐	☐	☐	☐
Self-Assessment Comments:	Is aware of: Strengths	☐	☐	☐	☐
	Needs	☐	☐	☐	☐
	Improvement/achievement	☐	☐	☐	☐
	Sets and implements learning goals	☐	☐	☐	☐
	Maintains logs, records, portfolio	☐	☐	☐	☐
	Works with others	☐	☐	☐	☐
	Shares ideas and materials	☐	☐	☐	☐
	Other:	☐	☐	☐	☐

Progress Report

Child's Name _____

At the top of the chart, record the book title, its grade/unit/week (for example, 1.2.3), and the child's accuracy percentage. See page 6 for measuring fluency, calculating accuracy and reading rates. At the bottom of the chart, record the date you took the running record. In the middle of the chart, make an X in the box across from the level of the child's reading—frustrational level (below 89% accuracy), instructional level (90–94% accuracy), or independent level (95–100% accuracy). Record the reading rate (WCPM) in the next row.

Book Title						
Grade/Unit/Week						
Reading Accuracy Percentage						
LEVEL — Frustrational (89% or below)						
LEVEL — Instructional (90–94%)						
LEVEL — Independent (95% or above)						
Reading Rate (WCPM)						
Date						

City Mouse and Country Mouse

SUMMARY Children compare life in the city to life in the country as they read a story about two mice. The characters' traits and observations drive the plot. In the end, both mice are happy to be back home.

LESSON VOCABULARY

beautiful	country
friend	someone
somewhere	

INTRODUCE THE BOOK

INTRODUCE THE TITLE AND AUTHOR Discuss the title and the author of *City Mouse and Country Mouse*. Ask children to look at the illustration of the two mice on the cover and identify the city mouse and the country mouse. Ask children how they know that the story is fiction.

BUILD BACKGROUND Prompt children to discuss other stories they have read where animal characters act like people. Help children distinguish between what is make-believe and what is similar to real life in the story. Look at the cover illustration together. Ask: Are there mice in the city and the country? Are the mice characters make-believe? How do you know? Do you think there are tall buildings in the city and rolling hills in the country? As we read, let's think about what is make-believe and what is similar to real life.

PREVIEW/USE ILLUSTRATIONS As children look through the book at the illustrations, encourage them to think about the genre, characters, and setting. Ask: Do you think this story could happen? Who are the most important characters? Where do you think the story takes place? How do you know?

READ THE BOOK

SET PURPOSE Model how to *set a purpose* for reading. Say: "I noticed from the illustration on the cover that City Mouse and Country Mouse are very different, yet they are both mice. I want to read to find out in what ways they are similar. As I read, I am going to look for traits that they share."

STRATEGY SUPPORT: PREDICT Review with children that making *predictions* is something they do everyday. They might predict what will happen during recess or after school. Explain that to make predictions about a story, children should pay attention to the details in the text. After the children read page 6, pause and ask them to predict what Country Mouse will do next. Lead children to recognize the pattern of events in the story.

COMPREHENSION QUESTIONS

PAGE 3 What did City Mouse and Country mouse first do together? *(They ate homemade soup.)*

PAGE 5 What is the main reason that City Mouse missed the city? *(There is a lot to do.)*

PAGE 6 How does the city make Country Mouse feel? *(tired)*

PAGE 7 In what settings did Country Mouse and City Mouse have fun? *(the country and the city)*

REVISIT THE BOOK

THINK AND SHARE

1. Characters—City Mouse and Country Mouse; setting—the city and the country.
2. Possible responses should show that children are able to confirm their predictions.
3. Possible response: My friend likes ice cream.
4. Possible response: Both have things to eat, fun things to do, and homes to live in.

EXTEND UNDERSTANDING Ask the children what happened in the story. Guide them to recognize what events happened at the beginning, the middle, and the end. Write the children's responses on separate pieces of paper. Then, ask them to put the events in order. Next, prompt children to think about how the traits of characters relate to the events. Ask such questions as, Why did City Mouse go to the country?

RESPONSE OPTIONS

WORD WORK Point out that the word *tired* is used twice in the story on pages 3 and 6. In each instance it has a different meaning. Ask children to look for context clues to understand the two meanings of *tired (bored, exhausted)*.

SOCIAL STUDIES CONNECTION

Students can find out what is special about their own communities by giving short oral reports about special places that they have visited, such as a park, zoo, children's museum, or beach.

Time For SOCIAL STUDIES

Skill Work

TEACH/REVIEW VOCABULARY

Play vocabulary memory. Write each word and its definition on separate index cards. Place them writing-side-down in rows. Have children take turns showing and reading two cards at a time. Children earn points by matching a word to its definition.

ELL Play vocabulary charades. Pair English language learners with proficient English speakers. Assign each pair of children a different vocabulary word. Give children time to decide how to act out the words.

TARGET SKILL AND STRATEGY

CHARACTER AND SETTING Explain to children that authors tell what the *characters* in the story are like. After children read page 3, pause and have them describe the traits of the two characters. Ask: What do the two mice like to do? What are they wearing? As children read, invite them to name any additional character traits. After reading, have children describe the *setting*. Explain that the setting is both the time and place of the story. The setting can be real or imaginary. Ask children to recall the two places in the story. Then ask them *when* the story took place. Ask: Is the time of the story a long time ago, or is it today?

PREDICT Remind children that when they know about the characters in a story, they can *predict* what the characters may think or do next. After children read to page 4, say: "We can predict that City Mouse and Country Mouse will go to the city, because Country Mouse says, 'Maybe the city is better.' Let's read to see if our prediction is right."

ADDITIONAL SKILL INSTRUCTION

THEME Describe *theme* as the big idea of the story. Discuss the theme by guiding children to notice how the feelings of Country Mouse and City Mouse changed during the story. Ask: What did they both learn from visiting each other's homes?

Character and Setting

Read the following paragraph from the story.
Write what you know about the setting.

> The very next day Country Mouse went to see her friend in the city. The mice went roller-skating on the sidewalk. They ate bread at a bakery. They heard someone sing at a club.

Setting:

_____   _____

- - - - - - - - - - - - - - - -   - - - - - - - - - - - - - - - -

_____   _____

- - - - - - - - - - - - - - - -   - - - - - - - - - - - - - - - -

_____   _____

Character:

Think about what you know about Country Mouse and City Mouse after reading the story. Match the characters to what each character likes.

Characters

I. Country Mouse

2. City Mouse

What Characters Like

a. the country best

b. the city best

c. peace and quiet

d. to do many things

e. to visit other places

Name _____

Vocabulary

Synonyms are words that have the same meaning. Draw a line to match the synonyms.

1. beautiful

2. country

3. friend

a. nation—a large group of people that share the same government

b. playmate—a child that plays with other children

c. pretty—pleasing to look at

4. Write a sentence with the word *someone*.

_____

_____

_____

5. Write a sentence with the word *somewhere*.

_____

_____

_____

Being an Astronaut

SUMMARY This nonfiction book explains what you need to know to be an astronaut. It extends the lesson concept of why someone would want to explore space.

LESSON VOCABULARY

everywhere	live
machines	move
woman	work
world	

INTRODUCE THE BOOK

INTRODUCE THE TITLE AND AUTHOR Discuss with children the title and author of *Being an Astronaut.* Explain that science includes learning about outer space. Ask: How does this book relate to science?

BUILD BACKGROUND Have children discuss what they know about astronauts. Ask: What does an astronaut do? Can anybody be an astronaut?

PREVIEW/USE TEXT FEATURES Have children look at the photos and read the headings and captions in the book before reading. Ask: What is special about the headings? (They are questions.)

READ THE BOOK

SET PURPOSE Have children set a purpose for reading *Being an Astronaut.* Remind children of what they discussed in the preview. You may need to work with children to have them set their own purposes. Ask: Would you like to learn what it means to be an astronaut?

STRATEGY SUPPORT: TEXT STRUCTURE Remind children that good readers look to see how an author organizes his or her ideas. Before, during, and after they read, children should think about the *text structure,* or pattern, that is used in a piece of writing. In the preview, have children read the headings. Have them identify the headings as being questions. Ask: Where are the answers to the questions? Guide children to see that the author has used a question-and-answer text structure. Explain that each heading covers a new topic. For example, on page 4, the topic is how astronauts eat. You can learn how they eat by reading the text. As they read *Being an Astronaut,* have children fill out the graphic organizer like the one in Think and Share. After reading, have children use the completed organizer to remember the basic points the author has made and to summarize the text.

COMPREHENSION QUESTIONS

PAGE 3 Is the first sentence a statement of fact, or a statement of opinion? Why? *(It is a statement of fact. It can be proved true or false.)*

PAGE 5 What is the main idea? *(Astronauts need to wear spacesuits.)*

PAGE 7 Why don't astronauts just do their experiments on Earth? *(Possible response: They want to see if things work differently in space.)*

PAGE 8 Why is it important for an astronaut to be able to call home? *(Possible response: They miss their families. They don't want loved ones to worry.)*

REVISIT THE BOOK

THINK AND SHARE

1. Astronauts live differently in space.
2. The author asked and answered questions about astronauts. Children's webs should include the questions in the book's headings.
3. Possible responses: *astronaut, spaceship, spacesuit*
4. Possible responses: Do you have to be a pilot or scientist to be an astronaut? Does space food taste like our food?

EXTEND UNDERSTANDING Have children examine the photos. Ask: What does the photo on page 4 show that is not explained in the text? Guide children to see how the photos add to their understanding of astronauts.

RESPONSE OPTIONS

WRITING Have children write a letter to an astronaut asking their questions from Think and Share.

SCIENCE CONNECTION

Display books and other information about space travel. Have children work in pairs to list differences between living in space and living on Earth.

TIME FOR Science

Skill Work

TEACH/REVIEW VOCABULARY

Give children sets of vocabulary word cards. Read clues aloud and have children hold up the matching word card. Possible clues: This means all over the place. This is the opposite of *die*. This is what you do to earn money. A mother is this. These help people do work. When you run, you do this. This is another word for *earth*.

ELL Help children make cards with vocabulary words on one side and the translations in their home languages on the other. Place the cards with the translation facing up and have children capture cards by naming the vocabulary words.

TARGET SKILL AND STRATEGY

MAIN IDEA AND DETAILS Tell children that a *topic* tells what a paragraph or article is about. The *main idea* is the most important idea about the *topic*. Sometimes the main idea is not given and children must state the main idea in their own words. Model using page 5: The topic here is spacesuits because the sentence and caption tell about astronauts and spacesuits. I think the main idea is *Astronauts need to wear spacesuits* because the details tell how spacesuits help astronauts live in space.

TEXT STRUCTURE Remind children to note the *text structure*, or pattern, used in a piece of writing. Guide children to see that the author has used a question-and-answer text structure where each question covers a new topic.

ADDITIONAL SKILL INSTRUCTION

FACT AND OPINION Remind children that a statement of *fact* can be proved true or false. Give these examples of statements of *fact*: "This is food." "I have a cat." A statement of *opinion* tells ideas or feelings, which cannot be proved true or false. Examples: This is the *worst* food." "My cat is *cuter* than yours."

Name _____

Main Idea and Details

Read the passage below.

Fill in the topic, the main idea, and two supporting details.

> Where do astronauts sleep?
> Some astronauts sleep in sleeping
> bags. Other astronauts sleep in bunks.
> Some just find a quiet spot to rest.

Topic

_____
- -
_____

Main Idea

_____
- -
_____

Supporting Details

_____   _____
- - - - - - - - - - - - - -   - - - - - - - - - - - - - -
_____   _____
- - - - - - - - - - - - - -   - - - - - - - - - - - - - -
_____   _____
- - - - - - - - - - - - - -   - - - - - - - - - - - - - -
_____   _____

Name _____

Vocabulary

Draw a line from each word to the word that means the opposite.

1. everywhere   a. man

2. live   b. nowhere

3. move   c. die

4. woman   d. stay

Write the words from the box to best complete the sentence.

Words to Know
machines   work   world

5. All around the _____, people

use _____ to help them

do their _____ .

Pup Camps Out

SUMMARY In this story, a puppy goes with his mother and father on his first camping trip. It extends the lesson concept of what we can discover by exploring nature.

LESSON VOCABULARY

bear	build
couldn't	father
love	mother
straight	

INTRODUCE THE BOOK

INTRODUCE THE TITLE AND AUTHOR Discuss with children the title and author of *Pup Camps Out*. Explain that science includes learning about how people relate to nature. Ask: How might this book connect to science?

BUILD BACKGROUND Ask children to share what they know about camping. Ask: How is camping different from living at home?

PREVIEW/USE TEXT FEATURES Have children look at the pictures in the book before reading. Ask: Who is the story about? What is happening? Have children read the heading for the background information on page 8. Ask and discuss: Is this part of the story? What is this part of the book about?

READ THE BOOK

SET PURPOSE Have children set a purpose for reading *Pup Camps Out*. Remind children of what they discussed in building background. You may need to work with children to have them set their own purpose. Ask: Do you want to know what Pup did while camping?

STRATEGY SUPPORT: MONITOR AND FIX UP

Remind children that good readers know that what they read must make sense. Tell children that they should check as they read this book to make sure they understand what they are reading. Model by reading page 3. Say: "This doesn't make sense. I want to know why Pup is so happy. Maybe I will find out later in the story." Model questions to ask: "What does this mean? Does this make sense? Do I understand this?" Explain that there are different ways to check understanding. One way is to read on. Model: "On page 6, Pup's father is thinking about a fish. Does this make sense? I should read on to find out why he did that." Encourage children to write short notes whenever there is something in the story they don't understand. Have them check off each note if it is cleared up later in the story.

COMPREHENSION QUESTIONS

PAGE 3 Why do you think Pup was happy? *(Possible response: He is having fun doing something new.)*

PAGE 4 Is this a realistic story or a fantasy? How can you tell? *(It's a fantasy. There are animals that talk.)*

PAGE 5 Which character trait describes Pup—helpful, shy, or hungry? *(helpful)*

PAGE 7 Why is Pup sleepy? *(He is tired from helping his parents and playing.)*

PAGE 7 Where did they go fishing? *(by a stream)*

REVISIT THE BOOK

THINK AND SHARE

1. Pup; He likes to learn new things and have fun.
2. Possible response: in the country; Pup learns about camping.
3. please, stream
4. Possible responses: It isn't safe for someone young like Pup to light a fire, put up a tent, scare a bear, or go fishing alone, but together with a parent, he can.

EXTEND UNDERSTANDING Have children analyze the story's plot. Remind children that a story's plot is what happens in the beginning, middle, and end of the story. Ask: What was the first thing that happened in the story? What happened next? How did the story end?

RESPONSE OPTIONS

VIEWING Have children write a sentence for each picture in the story describing what happened in that picture.

SCIENCE CONNECTION

Display books and other information about camping. Have children list things they should do to protect camping areas, such as extinguishing campfires, respecting animals, and disposing of trash.

Skill Work

TEACH/REVIEW VOCABULARY

Give each child a set of vocabulary word cards. Write these word groups on the board: *can't, could've, _____; enjoy, like, _____; make, create, _____; dad, daddy, _____; fox, wolf, _____; mom, mommy, _____; even, in line, _____.* Read each group aloud, and have children show the word that belongs.

TARGET SKILL AND STRATEGY

CHARACTER AND SETTING Tell children that *characters* are the people or animals in stories. Authors describe their characters, telling what they look like, how they act, and what kind of people they are. As they read, have children answer questions about each character. Next, tell children that the *setting* is the time and place of a story. After children have identified the main place, ask them to identify the season. As they read, have children tell how the specific setting changes from page to page.

ELL Give each child a word web for each character. Have them fill in character traits for Pup, Mother Dog, and Father Dog as they read the story.

MONITOR AND FIX UP Remind children to check as they read to make sure they understand the text. Explain that they may reread to clear up any confusion. Remind children that checking their understanding and rereading will make it easier to understand the characters and the setting in the story.

ADDITIONAL SKILL INSTRUCTION

REALISM AND FANTASY Remind children that a *realistic story* tells about something that could happen. A *fantasy* is a make-believe story. As they read *Pup Camps Out*, model questions to ask, such as: Do animals talk in the story? Is there magic in the story? Do the people in the story do and say things like people I know? Near the end, ask: Is this a realistic story or a fantasy?

Name _____

Character and Setting

Read each sentence below. Then circle the answer that best completes each sentence.

1. When Pup asked Father Dog to teach him, he was by the

   a. car.　　　　　　b. tent.　　　　　　c. house.

2. The story happened

   a. at night.　　　b. 100 years ago.　　c. in the present day.

3. Mother Dog

   a. likes to camp.　　b. stayed at home.　　c. is reading a book.

4. Father Dog is

   a. wise.　　　　　　b. forgetful.　　　　c. angry.

5. Write a sentence about Pup.

   _____

   _____

   _____

Name _____

Vocabulary

Draw a line from each word at the left to the word or words at the right that mean the same.

1. build   **a.** dad

2. father   **b.** care about

3. love   **c.** mom

4. mother   **d.** make

Complete the sentence using the words from the box.

Words to Know
bear   couldn't   straight

5. The big _____ was strong, but he _____

run in a _____ line.

Desert

SUMMARY This nonfiction book involves use of all the senses as it describes the climate, animals, and plants in the desert.

LESSON VOCABULARY

animals	early
eyes	full
warm	water

INTRODUCE THE BOOK

INTRODUCE THE TITLE AND AUTHOR Discuss with children the title and author of *Desert*. Based on the title and cover photograph, ask children about the first thing that comes to their minds when they think of deserts. Talk about what sand looks and feels like. Ask if they think anything grows in sand. Suggest they read and find out.

BUILD BACKGROUND If possible, have a flat box of sand and a cactus on hand. Invite children to feel the sand and carefully touch the cactus. Invite children to imagine walking in sand for many days. Ask for volunteers to share their "experiences" in the desert, if any.

PREVIEW/TAKE A PICTURE WALK As children look through the book, draw their attention to the various text features, including photographs and captions. Read a caption, and explain to children why it is interesting to you. Ask them to do the same as they go through the book.

READ THE BOOK

SET PURPOSE Ask: Do you like to hear the sound of a rattlesnake or feel cool water run on your face when it's hot? Let children know that the desert has many sights and sounds. Encourage children to set their own purposes for reading a book about the desert.

STRATEGY SUPPORT: TEXT STRUCTURE After children have read the book, ask them to list all the ideas that come to mind when they think of sand. Show them how to put these ideas into a graphic organizer. Then suggest they write one sentence about desert sand.

COMPREHENSION QUESTIONS

PAGE 3 What is one way of finding out what the desert is like? *(You can read about life in the desert.)*

PAGES 5–6 What animals might you see in the desert? *(prairie dogs, rattlesnakes, lizards, and coyotes)*

PAGE 7 Why does the cactus do well in the desert? *(They can store water.)*

PAGE 8 Why must you bring water when you go to the desert? *(It is very dry.)*

REVISIT THE BOOK

THINK AND SHARE

1. Possible response: The desert is dry, but it still has a lot of animal and plant life.
2. Possible responses: Questions: What would you see in the desert? What would you hear in the desert? What is the weather in the desert? Answers: prairie dogs, flowers, cactuses; rattlesnake's tail, coyote's howl; dry
3. *flying, digging, shaking, running, howling; fly, dig, shake, run, howl*
4. barn owl, rattlesnake, prairie dog, coyote, horned lizard

EXTEND UNDERSTANDING Invite children to pick one sense to describe the plants and animals of the desert. Suggest that they show animals or plants they are interested in by drawing their own desert scene. Then children can make up captions to describe their scenes. For example: *The cactuses look like they are reaching for the sky. The howl of the coyote sounds sad.*

RESPONSE OPTIONS

WORD WORK Start a list titled, *Things I Like About Sand.* Have children choose favorites, and write the words on strips of paper. Stand them in your box of sand—the "Word Desert."

SCIENCE CONNECTION

Ask children to choose one animal from those shown in the book. Have them read in other texts and on the Internet about that animal and talk with a partner about how the animal survives in the desert.

Skill Work

TEACH/REVIEW VOCABULARY

Display pictures representing the five senses. Form a group for each sense. Ask each group to come up with sentences in which they relate the vocabulary words to their sense. For example, the group for the sense of touch can say how good *water* feels after days in the dry desert.

ELL Give children sets of vocabulary word cards. Have them write clue words or phrases on the backs. Suggest that the clues relate to the senses.

TARGET SKILL AND STRATEGY

MAIN IDEA AND DETAILS Explain to children that they will be looking for the *main idea* of this book about the desert. Remind them that the main idea is the most important idea about the topic (the desert). As they read facts about the desert, help them organize the information so that they can figure out the main idea. Help them understand that while a desert may look like a lot of sand, it is a place full of variety in plant and animal life.

TEXT STRUCTURE The descriptions of life in the desert form the *text structure* and can be grouped around each sense. Make a five-column chart using each of the senses as a column heading, with the word *Desert* as the title. Ask children to tell you what you can see, hear, smell, touch, or taste in the desert, and put each item in its proper column.

ADDITIONAL SKILL INSTRUCTION

COMPARE AND CONTRAST Use the five senses to help children compare and contrast. Ask: How is seeing a rattlesnake different from hearing one? How is tasting water like seeing water? Since there are no clue words, guide children to understand how our senses are alike and different when we use them in the desert.

Name _____

Main Idea and Details

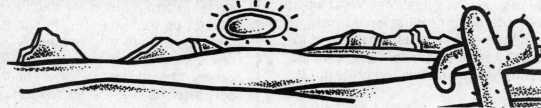

1. Write one word that tells
    the topic of this book.

    _____
    -
    _____

2. Choose the main idea—the most important idea about the
    desert—and circle it.

    > All deserts have lots of sand.
    >
    > The desert can be hot and dry, but it has
    > many plants and animals.
    >
    > The desert prairie dog lives with rattlesnakes
    > and cactuses.

3. What are some details that tell more about the main idea?
    Choose two detail sentences from the box and circle them.

    > You can see and hear different animals.
    >
    > I went to the desert.
    >
    > Many flowers and trees grow in the
    > dry desert.
    >
    > It always rains in the desert.

Name _____

Vocabulary

Circle the letter that begins each word.
Write the letter on the line.

Words to Know

animals	early	eyes
full	warm	water

b a

1. _____ nimals

e a

2. _____ ye

s e

3. _____ arly

w t

4. _____ arm

r w

5. _____ ater

f t

6. _____ ull

7. Write a sentence about the desert using one or more words
from the box.

_____

_____

_____

The Case of the Missing Fish

◎ REALISM AND FANTASY
◎ MONITOR AND FIX UP

SUMMARY This play presents a brief story of Bird's search for Fish. He asks several animals before finding Elephant, who helps him see the answer.

LESSON VOCABULARY

gone	learn	often
pieces	though	together
very		

INTRODUCE THE BOOK

INTRODUCE THE TITLE AND AUTHOR Discuss with children the title and the author of *The Case of the Missing Fish.* Based on the title and cover illustration, ask them what they think this play will be about and what characters they think they will find in it.

BUILD BACKGROUND Ask the children to talk about plays: Have they ever seen one? What are they like? How are they different from reading a story? Lead children to talk about a play with characters who act out the story. Point out that the characters seem to be talking animals. Use this suggestion to begin a later discussion about distinguishing fantasy and realism.

PREVIEW/USE TEXT FEATURES Help the children look through the play and notice that each character's part is identified. Ask them who they think the main character is. There may be some disagreement as to whether it is Bird or Fish. Explain that there may be two main characters.

READ THE BOOK

SET PURPOSE Let the children know how much fun it is to put on a play because everyone works together. Suggest that they make some masks or props that will make this play more effective. The natural excitement of a play may help the children to set their own purpose for reading this book.

STRATEGY SUPPORT: MONITOR AND FIX UP Even though this plot is easy for the children to follow, it is still important for them to identify any problems they may have in reading it. When you discuss what happened when Fish had left his tank, point out to the children that they are using their own thinking skills to figure out "a case" and to decide if this play is a fantasy or a realistic story. The children should see that the animals in this play used thinking skills to solve the case just as the children use their thinking skills.

COMPREHENSION QUESTIONS

PAGE 4 Why was it important that Squirrel heard a splash? (*It made Bird think more about where Fish could be.*)

PAGE 5 What clue did Zebra give for finding Fish? (*He said it was Tuesday.*)

PAGE 5 Why was Bird interested in the splash and what Fish had said? (*He knew they were clues to where Fish was.*)

PAGE 6 What does Elephant figure out? (*Fish often takes a bath on Tuesday.*)

REVISIT THE BOOK

THINK AND SHARE

1. The animal characters talk and act like people.
2. Squirrel and Zebra; the animals' names are in dark letters, followed by a colon, and come before their lines.
3. Possible responses: We work together. These pieces are part of a whole. We learn at school. I often ride my bike.
4. Responses will vary.

EXTEND UNDERSTANDING The children may want to make up their own play using animals as characters. Help them to come up with a problem, similar to the missing fish, to be the main problem of the play. Ask them about the setting and whether they will need any props. Encourage them to write a play.

RESPONSE OPTIONS

WORD WORK Review the consonant digraphs *sh, th,* and *ph* with the children. Have them look through the book for examples of these sounds at the beginning or end of words, such as in *the* and *fish* in the title and *splash* on page 4. Ask them to think of other words that they often use with those sounds (for example, *dish, phone,* and *then*).

SOCIAL STUDIES CONNECTION

Time For SOCIAL STUDIES

The underlying thread in this play is how Bird kept asking questions until he found the answer. Remind the children that there are many places to look when we have questions. Ask them to suggest what some resources are for answering our questions. Write a list on the board as they respond. At a later time, help volunteers demonstrate use of the suggested resources. Tell them not to forget thinking skills, which Bird used, to find answers to questions.

TEACH/REVIEW VOCABULARY

Many of the vocabulary words describe abstract ideas (*learn, often, though, together, very*). Together with the children, write a sentence for each word. Ask questions such as: Why do you say, "I go to the store *often?*" How does the word *often* change the sentence?

ELL In pairs, have more proficient English speakers say a sentence frame that leaves out a vocabulary word; have English language learners fill in the correct word. After all words have been covered once, reverse roles.

TARGET SKILL AND STRATEGY

REALISM AND FANTASY Help the children distinguish between a *realistic* story and a *fantasy* by asking if this story could really happen. On the board write: *This Could Happen* and *This Could Not Happen.* Have the children say what could happen and what could not happen, and list their responses under the appropriate heading. Discuss why this play is a fantasy.

MONITOR AND FIX UP *Monitoring* their reading can help readers understand why Squirrel says he heard a splash. Model how children should stop, identify that they have a problem in understanding, and reread the page or read on to clear things up. This skill can help children understand if they are reading about something that could happen (realistic story) or a fantasy.

ADDITIONAL SKILL INSTRUCTION

CAUSE AND EFFECT Make a two-column chart on the board with labels *What happened* and *Why it happened.* Guide the children to list pairs of events from the story under the headings. Reread with them pages 4–5 to see that once Bird was told that Squirrel heard a splash and that Fish said it was Tuesday (why it happened), he was well on his way to finding Fish (what happened).

Realism and Fantasy

A **fantasy** is a story about something that could not happen.
A **realistic story** tells about something that could happen.

Read the sentences.
Write R on the line if the sentences begin a realistic story
or F if they begin a fantasy.

_____

_____ 1. Once upon a time there lived three little pigs.
One wanted to build a house out of straw.

_____ 2. Fish said to Bird, "I often take a bath on Tuesday."

_____ 3. Tom never wanted to hunt bears. He always loved
bears. So he asked his dad to stop hunting bears.

_____ 4. Long ago, in a faraway land, lived a girl with a red
coat and hood. Her mother asked her to visit her
grandmother. On the way, a wolf asked her where
she was going.

_____ 5. A long, long time ago dinosaurs walked all over Earth.
Some people have found huge footprints left by
dinosaurs.

Name _____

Vocabulary

Read each sentence. Choose the best word to finish the sentence and circle it.

Words to Know

| gone | learn | often | pieces |
| though | together | very | |

1. Sam had many _____ of paper.
   stack   pieces

2. LaToya could _____ well from this tutor.
   teach   learn

3. Sherry wanted to go out, even _____ it was raining.
   through   though

4. Sandy went to the park _____ with her friends.
   together   alone

5. Nancy _____ goes to the store for her mom.
   cannot   often

6. All the students except Hank had _____ home.
   gone   mine

7. Elephant said he loved playing ball _____ much.
   not   very

8. Write a sentence that Fish might say to Bird. Use a vocabulary word in your sentence.

_____

_____

_____

Dogs to the Rescue

SUMMARY This book shows children how dogs can be more than just pets. It describes of the typical training of a rescue dog and provides photographs to support children's comprehension.

LESSON VOCABULARY

break	family
heard	listen
once	pull

INTRODUCE THE BOOK

INTRODUCE THE TITLE AND AUTHOR Discuss with children the title and the author of *Dogs to the Rescue*. Have children describe the cover and how it relates to the title. Ask them what topics may be covered in the book.

BUILD BACKGROUND Discuss the dangers from which people often need to be rescued, such as floods, fires, or earthquakes. Have dog owners tell about the unique characteristics of dogs, such as their loyalty and sense of smell.

PREVIEW/USE TEXT FEATURES Ask children to look through the book at the photographs and captions. Ask: How do the photographs and captions help you to predict what the book will be about?

READ THE BOOK

SET PURPOSE Have children set a purpose for reading by thinking of one question about rescue dogs to be answered by reading this book. Remind children as they read to look for the answers to their questions.

STRATEGY SUPPORT: PREDICT Review with children other ways that *predicting* can be helpful before and during reading. Remind them that when they preview, they should make predictions about what the book will be about. When children read page 3, pause and encourage them to predict what they think they will read about on the next page. Lead children to predict they will read about how rescue dogs help rescue workers. Write their predictions on the board. As children continue to read, take note when their predictions are confirmed.

COMPREHENSION QUESTIONS

PAGE 3 How do rescue workers help others? *(They bring people to safety.)*

PAGE 4 What is the most important idea in the paragraph? *(Rescue dogs help people.)*

PAGE 6 What do families that take in rescue dogs need to know? *(how to train a rescue dog)*

PAGE 7 In your own words, when is a rescue dog ready to work? *(after it learns to follow the important commands)*

PAGE 8 What facts support the idea that rescue dogs have happy and busy lives? *(Rescue dogs are trained with families. They help people in many ways.)*

REVISIT THE BOOK

THINK AND SHARE

1. Possible response: First, a family takes the puppy home. Next, the dog learns to listen and follow commands. Finally, the dog can work with a rescue worker.
2. Possible response: to practice going into difficult places
3. Possible response: The dog will be healthy and happy.
4. Answers will vary. Possible response: Yes, because a dog can sometimes go where humans cannot go.

EXTEND UNDERSTANDING The photographs on pages 4 and 5 can help children visualize how rescue dogs and rescue workers work as a team. Ask: From looking at the photographs and reading the captions, what can rescue dogs do that humans cannot? How do you think a rescue dog communicates to the rescue worker? Do you think rescue dogs are generally kept on a leash? Do you think the rescue workers care for and respect their rescue dogs? Would you like to work with animals someday?

RESPONSE OPTIONS

WRITING Ask children to write one fact and one opinion about rescue dogs.

ELL Lead a writing activity that uses sentence frames such as: *Rescue dogs are _____. Rescue dogs can _____. Rescue dogs have _____.* Direct the children to copy and complete the sentences on their own papers.

SOCIAL STUDIES CONNECTION

Time For SOCIAL STUDIES

Children may want to find out more about how dogs help people everyday. Arrange with the librarian to have some books in the classroom about service dogs, sled dogs, and herding dogs.

Skill Work

TEACH/REVIEW VOCABULARY

Remind children that when they come to an unfamiliar word, they can look at its sentence and its surrounding sentences for clues to its meaning. Direct children to find the word *break* on page 7. Ask a volunteer to explain the meaning of the word. Then ask what surrounding words or sentences gave clues to the meaning. Repeat the process with each vocabulary word.

TARGET SKILL AND STRATEGY

SEQUENCE Remind children that it is important to keep track of the *sequence*, or order of events, when reading. As they read about rescue dogs and their training on pages 6 and 7, ask children to point to the sentence that tells what the dogs learn first, next, and last. Point out the clue words *once* and *when*.

PREDICT Children can draw upon their prior knowledge to *predict* what will come next in the sequence of topics in a book. Explain that predicting is thinking about what will probably happen next. As children come to page 6, tell them to close their books and ask: What information do you think will be next in the book? Write children's predictions on the board and have children read on to *confirm* them. Explain: Pausing to predict when reading lets you self-check your comprehension.

ADDITIONAL SKILL INSTRUCTION

FACT AND OPINION As children finish reading, review that *opinions* are ideas that express a person's feelings or beliefs, while *facts* can be proved true or false. Ask children to write down their own opinions about rescue dogs. Allow time for children to share their opinions with the class. Point out clue words that express opinion, such as the verbs *think*, *feel*, and *believe*.

Name_____

Sequence

Sequence refers to the order of events in both fiction and nonfiction. Sequence can also refer to the steps in a process.

Read the passage in the box. Then read what happens next. Put the sentences in order by writing the correct number from 1–5 next to each sentence.

Rachel went for a walk in the forest. She tripped and fell on a rock. Her ankle hurt, so she could not walk back to her car. She used her cell phone to call for help. A rescue worker named Miguel was sent to the forest to help Rachel.

_____ Miguel looks at Rachel's leg to see if it is broken.

_____ Next, Rachel smiles when she sees Miguel and Max.

_____ After Max picks up Rachel's smell, he follows a path into the woods.

_____ Then Max stops and holds up his head. Max and Miguel hear Rachel cry for help.

_____ First, Miguel and his rescue dog Max find Rachel's car.

Name_____

Vocabulary

Unscramble each word below. Look at the words in the box to help you. Write the word on the line.
Say the word aloud. Count the number of syllables.

Words to Know
break   family   heard   listen   once   pull

1. ymifal _____   How many syllables? _____

2. draeh _____   How many syllables? _____

3. enltis _____   How many syllables? _____

4. lpul _____   How many syllables? _____

5. ceon _____   How many syllables? _____

6. akbre _____   How many syllables? _____

7. Write a sentence using one of the vocabulary words.

_____

_____

_____

Let's Play Baseball!

SUMMARY Boys and girls play an exciting baseball game together and show good sportsmanship. Readers' experiences playing sports bring this story to life.

LESSON VOCABULARY

certainly	either
great	laugh
second	worst
you're	

INTRODUCE THE BOOK

INTRODUCE THE TITLE AND AUTHOR Discuss the title and the author of *Let's Play Baseball!* Ask children if they think the book is fiction or nonfiction. Encourage class discussion about the illustration on the cover.

BUILD BACKGROUND Review with children the basic rules and terms of baseball. Draw a baseball diamond on the board. Ask volunteers to help you fill out the names of positions and bases. Ask: Where does the pitcher stand? Where is home plate? What is an inning and how many are there in a game?

PREVIEW/TAKE A PICTURE WALK As children look through the book at the illustrations, have them think about the characters and their actions. Ask: How many coaches are there? What position does the coach play in the game? Look at pages 4–5. Ask a volunteer to describe what is happening in the game.

READ THE BOOK

SET PURPOSE Have children set a purpose for reading by looking at the cover illustration. Guide them to think of one question about the characters, the game of baseball, or the story to answer as they read.

STRATEGY SUPPORT: PRIOR KNOWLEDGE As children finish reading page 5, pause and model how to connect the text to their prior knowledge. Say: This part of the book reminds me of when I played baseball. Remembering my experiences playing baseball makes the story more exciting. I can appreciate how hard it is to hit a fast ball and to run to second base. Pause again on page 7, and ask children if any part of the story reminds them of their own experiences. Ask: Has anyone played a close game in any sport? How did it feel when you won? How did it feel when you lost?

COMPREHENSION QUESTIONS

PAGE 3 Where is second base? *(Possible response: behind the pitcher)*

PAGE 4 Why did Jill continue to run after she reached first base? *(Possible response: because the ball was not picked up yet)*

PAGE 5 What does the word *safe* mean in baseball? *(Possible response: It means that she reached the base without being tagged out.)*

PAGE 6 In baseball, how many players from one team have to make outs for the other team to be up at bat? *(three players)*

REVISIT THE BOOK

THINK AND SHARE

1. Possible response: This story is a realistic story because kids do play baseball. The actions and feelings of the players really could happen.
2. Possible response: It tells about the rules.
3. let's/let us, you're/you are, you'll/you will, it's/it is, who's/who is, can't/can not
4. Possible response: Playing baseball is fun even if you don't win.

EXTEND UNDERSTANDING Ask children to think about who is telling the story. On page 3, the coach is talking to a person who refers to himself as "me." Ask: Can you find clues on the other pages that show who is telling the story? Do you see who it might be in the pictures? Ask a volunteer to reveal the storyteller and explain how he or she knew. Help children understand the concept if they have difficulty by pointing out the phrase "I catch the ball" on page 5 or "I hit a home run!" on page 7. Explain that sometimes a character in the story acts as the storyteller, while other times stories are written as if someone were watching the action through a window.

RESPONSE OPTIONS

WRITING Have children write two sentences describing what makes a good teammate.

SOCIAL STUDIES CONNECTION

Time For SOCIAL STUDIES

Have children go to the library and choose books about their favorite sports. Have each child present to the class one fact he or she knew before reading the book and one fact they learned from the book.

Skill Work

TEACH/REVIEW VOCABULARY

Write a sentence for each vocabulary word on the board such as: *Our team came in ____ (second) place in the relay race.* Next to the sentences, in a different order, write the vocabulary words. Ask volunteers to write the correct word in the space provided.

ELL Help children think of synonyms or simple definitions for the vocabulary words. Have them make cards for each word and each definition. Arrange cards face down and have children take turns showing two cards at a time, trying to match words and meanings.

TARGET SKILL AND STRATEGY

REALISM AND FANTASY Before reading, remind children that fiction can be realistic stories or fantasies. A *realistic* story is something that could happen. A *fantasy* is something that could not happen. Ask children to look at the cover illustration to predict what type of story *Let's Play Baseball!* is. Guide them to support their answers with specific details.

PRIOR KNOWLEDGE Explain that *prior knowledge* can help students figure out whether a story is realistic or a fantasy. Point out that prior knowledge can be from students' own experiences, from reading, or from what others have taught them.

ADDITIONAL SKILL INSTRUCTION

LITERARY ELEMENTS Write *Setting* at the top of the board with the questions "Where?" and "When?" Next, write *Characters* with the question "Who?" Then write *Plot* with the question "What happened?" and the words "Beginning," "Middle," and "End." Write children's responses next to the appropriate question.

Name _____

Realism and Fantasy

Think about the story *Let's Play Baseball!* Write
realistic story or *fantasy* to answer the questions below.

I. If the character Sam were a rabbit, would the story be a
realistic story or a fantasy?

_____

_____

2. If the character Ann had hit a home run, would the story be a
realistic story or a fantasy?

_____

_____

3. If the children had played baseball on the moon, would the
story be a realistic story or a fantasy?

_____

_____

4. If Sam's team had lost the game, would the story be a realistic
story or a fantasy?

_____

_____

5. If they had come to the baseball field riding elephants, would
the story be a realistic story or a fantasy?

_____

_____

Name _____

Vocabulary

Draw a line to match the word to its meaning.

Words to Know

certainly	either	great	laugh
second	worst	you're	

1. certainly

2. either

3. great

4. laugh

5. second

6. you're

7. worst

a. one or the other

b. without a doubt

c. a sound you make when something is funny

d. you are

e. the next after first

f. very good

g. the most bad

Synonyms are words that have the same meaning.
Draw a line to match the synonyms.

8. laugh

9. great

10. certainly

h. surely

i. giggle

j. terrific

Busy Beavers

SUMMARY This nonfiction book describes how beavers build a home in a stream. It extends the lesson concept of what we can share.

LESSON VOCABULARY

above	ago
enough	toward
whole	word

INTRODUCE THE BOOK

INTRODUCE THE TITLE AND AUTHOR Discuss with children the title and the author of *Busy Beavers*. Explain that science includes learning how different animals live in their environments. Ask: How might this book relate to science?

BUILD BACKGROUND Have children discuss what they know about what lives and grows in or along streams. Have children also share anything they may know about beavers.

PREVIEW/TAKE A PICTURE WALK Have children look at the photographs in the book before reading. Ask: What are the beavers doing in these photographs? What do you think happens first, next, and last based on the pictures?

READ THE BOOK

SET PURPOSE Have children set a purpose for reading *Busy Beavers*. Remind them of what they discussed when previewing the photographs. You may need to work with children to have them set their own purposes. Ask: Would you like to know how beavers build their homes?

STRATEGY SUPPORT: SUMMARIZE Remind children that good readers are able to use their own words to tell the important things that happen in a book or what the book is about. Using their own words to retell is a way of showing that they understand what they have read. Model summarizing page 4: On this page, I read that beavers use their sharp teeth to cut down trees. Then they cut off the branches and bark and carry the logs to the river. To tell what happens in my own words, I ask, "What is this page mostly about?" I will use my own words to tell: "Beavers use their teeth to make logs." As children read *Busy Beavers,* have them tell the main idea of each page by asking: What is this page mostly about?

COMPREHENSION QUESTIONS

PAGE 3 Is the last sentence a statement of fact or a statement of opinion? Why? *(It is a statement of fact. It can be proved true or false.)*

PAGES 4–5 What happens first, next, and last? *(First: Beavers cut down trees. Next: They cut off the branches. Next: They cut off the bark. Last: They use mud to glue it all together.)*

PAGE 7 What must a beaver be able to do well? *(swim)*

PAGE 8 How do the kits stay safe? *(Possible response: They are inside the lodge.)*

REVISIT THE BOOK

THINK AND SHARE

1. cut down trees, cut off branches and bark, move logs, glue with mud
2. Possible response: Beavers work together to build safe homes on the stream.
3. *ar: hard, sharp, bark; or: order, for, born*
4. Possible responses: It keeps them dry. It is hard for other animals to get inside.

EXTEND UNDERSTANDING Have children examine the photographs. Ask: What do you see in the photographs that is not explained in the words? Guide children to see how the photographs add to their understanding of beavers.

RESPONSE OPTIONS

WRITING Have children write one or two sentences that describe a beaver lodge.

SCIENCE CONNECTION

TIME FOR Science

Display information about where river turtles and frogs rest. Have children work in pairs to make charts for comparing beaver, turtle, and frog homes.

Skill Work

TEACH/REVIEW VOCABULARY

Give pairs of children a set of vocabulary word cards and another set with the words' definitions. Have pairs play a memory game by matching each word to its definition.

ELL Help children make word cards with a vocabulary word on one side and a translation in their home language on the other side. Lay out the cards, translation side up, and have children capture cards by naming the vocabulary words.

TARGET SKILL AND STRATEGY

SEQUENCE Remind children to think about what happens first, next, and last as they read. Point out the words *first, next,* and *then* on page 4. Explain that these clue words tell the order of steps that beavers use to prepare logs. Have children use a sequence ladder to map the sequence of events described on pages 4–5.

SUMMARIZE Tell children they should be able to tell in their own words what happens in a book. Remind them that if they can use their own words to tell what a book is about, it will be easier to tell what happens first, next, and last.

ADDITIONAL SKILL INSTRUCTION

FACT AND OPINION Remind children that a statement of *fact* tells something that can be proved true or false by checking it with another book, an expert, or the Internet. A statement of *opinion* tells ideas or feelings. It cannot be proved true or false. Have children read the first sentence on page 4. Explain that this is a statement of fact, because it can be proved true or false. Give these examples of statements of opinion: This is the *best* book. *Everyone* likes popcorn. Encourage children to continue to identify statements in the book.

Name _____

Sequence

Read the passage. The beavers did things in a certain order.
Underline the clue words that help you know that order.
Write what the beavers did next to the clue words below.

Beavers have strong, sharp teeth. First, they use their teeth to cut down trees. Next, they cut off the branches. Then they cut off the bark. The beavers then carry the logs toward the stream.

I. First _____
_____
_____.

2. Next _____
_____
_____.

3. Then _____
_____
_____.

4. Last _____
_____
_____.

Name _____

Vocabulary

Write the words from the word box that fit in the puzzle below. Some letters have been done for you. When you are finished, the letters in the dark boxes will spell an important word from the book.

Words to Know
above   ago   enough   toward   whole   word

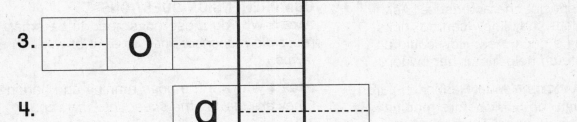

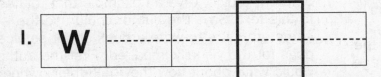

1. W
2. r
3. o
4. a
5. g

Write a word from the word box to complete the sentence.

6. Part of the beaver's lodge is _____ the water.

Dogs at Work

SUMMARY Read about how border collies keep farm animals safe and in order. The author chooses interesting facts to express affection toward dogs. Descriptive text helps children visualize the everyday life of a dog at work.

LESSON VOCABULARY

bought	people
pleasant	probably
scared	shall
sign	

INTRODUCE THE BOOK

INTRODUCE THE TITLE AND AUTHOR Discuss the title and the author of *Dogs at Work*. Invite children to comment on the photograph on the cover and how it relates to the title. Encourage them to predict what social studies topic may be covered in the book.

BUILD BACKGROUND Invite children to talk about dogs and their special characteristics. Ask children if the dogs they know can do tricks such as fetching a stick. Ask: How could a dog's ability to fetch help his or her owner?

PREVIEW/TAKE A PICTURE WALK Remind children to browse through the book before reading and to look at the pictures. Prompt children to predict what the book will be about. Ask: What other animals are shown? Do the dogs seem friendly or dangerous?

READ THE BOOK

SET PURPOSE Ask children how the title *Dogs at Work* and previewing the photographs help them set a purpose for reading. Lead them to predict what kind of work dogs can do and to read to find out if their predictions are correct.

STRATEGY SUPPORT: TEXT STRUCTURE Reinforce for children the importance of text structure to a reader. Explain that the way an author organizes information can help them make sense of what they read. Different stories can have a similar structure but be about different topics. Give an example that relates to this text. Say: The author could use the same structure to write a book about service dogs for the visually impaired. First the author would write about how they help their owners. What do you think the author would write about next?

COMPREHENSION QUESTIONS

PAGE 3 Why do these dogs need to be smart? *(Possible response: They do a lot of work on farms.)*

PAGE 4 Why are the dogs running and barking? *(They are moving the sheep into the pen.)*

PAGE 6 Are border collies born knowing how to work on a farm? *(No, they will learn how to help.)*

PAGE 7 What is the dog doing in the picture? *(Possible response: playing with the cat)*

PAGE 8 Why do you think border collies make good companions to the farmers? *(Possible response: They are friendly and like working.)*

REVISIT THE BOOK

THINK AND SHARE

1. Possible response: The author wanted to teach people about dogs at work.
2. Possible response: by herding and protecting other farm animals
3. Singular: sign, pen, farmer; Plural: farms, dogs, animals
4. Possible response: both, because they are friends and helpers to the farmer

EXTEND UNDERSTANDING When children come to pages 4 and 5, pause and tell them to study the pictures. Ask: How do these pictures help you understand how dogs help farmers? Where do you think the farmer needs the animals moved to and from? Why? Why would moving herds of animals be difficult for the farmer to do by himself?

RESPONSE OPTIONS

WRITING Review facts with the children—working dogs herd, protect, run, and play. Ask children to write two sentences that describe the dogs' most important job on the farm.

ELL Have children draw pictures of farms. Ask them to label what they included in their drawings.

SOCIAL STUDIES CONNECTION

Time For
SOCIAL
STUDIES

Have your librarian suggest a selection of fables and other tales based on the theme of animals helping people. Make the books available for children to read independently, or read a few to the class.

Skill Work

TEACH/REVIEW VOCABULARY

Lead a synonym activity. First, describe synonyms as words with the same meaning. Assign pairs of children vocabulary words and their synonyms: *people/humans, sign/signal, shall/will, bought/purchased, pleasant/nice, scared/frightened*. Have each pair of children write a sentence that uses the synonym. Then have the group replace the synonym with the vocabulary word.

TARGET SKILL AND STRATEGY

AUTHOR'S PURPOSE Ask children to identify the author of this book. Before reading, ask: What do you think the book will be about? Why? How do you think you will feel about working dogs after reading this book? Do you think this book is funny, sad, serious, or exciting? Have children explain their answers.

TEXT STRUCTURE Noticing the *text structure* can help children identify the author's purpose. Ask children what facts they learned about farm dogs. Write each fact in a concept web. Help children see that each fact describes a different activity. Ask: Why do you think the author chose to write about these facts? How did learning these facts make you feel about working dogs?

ADDITIONAL SKILL INSTRUCTION

VISUALIZE Model *visualizing* using page 4. Tell children that as they read they should form pictures in their minds about what is happening in the text. Say: When I read this page, I can see a picture in my mind of a dog running behind a herd of sheep heading toward a pen. If a sheep moves out of the herd, the dog runs up to it, barks, and guides it back.

Name _____

Author's Purpose

Read the text below. Then circle the best answer for each question.

> Border collies love to work. They also like to run and play. They have a good time. It is probably lots of fun for them to live and work on the farm!

1. Why did the author write about what these dogs like to do?
   a. to teach
   b. to be funny
   c. to be sad

2. What is another reason the author wrote about what border collies like to do?
   a. so that you will like the story
   b. so that you will like the author
   c. so that you will not like dogs

3. How does the author want you to feel about a farm dog's life?
   a. that it is hard
   b. that it is bad
   c. that it is fun

4. Write a sentence that tells what you think about border collies after reading the book.

_____
- - - - - - - - - - - - - - - - - - - -
_____
- - - - - - - - - - - - - - - - - - - -
_____
- - - - - - - - - - - - - - - - - - - -
_____

Name _____

Vocabulary

Draw a line to match the word to its meaning.

Words to Know
bought   people   pleasant   probably
scared   shall   sign

---

1. bought

2. sign

3. shall

4. probably

5. pleasant

6. scared

a. nice, pleasing

b. afraid

c. got something by paying money

d. likely to happen or be true

e. a helping verb sometimes used in place of *will* or *should*

f. a symbol or hand movement that means something

---

7. Choose two words from the box and write a sentence for each.

_____

- -

_____

- -

_____

- -

_____

Together for Thanksgiving

SUMMARY This story describes a typical Thanksgiving Day. Relatives and friends gather for the feast, and everyone brings a different kind of food. When dinner is served, everyone says what they are thankful for. After dinner, everyone goes outside and plays ball. At the end of the day, everyone is sorry to go.

LESSON VOCABULARY

behind	brought
door	everybody
minute	promise
sorry	

INTRODUCE THE BOOK

INTRODUCE THE TITLE AND AUTHOR Discuss with children the title and the author of *Together for Thanksgiving*. Based on the title, ask children what they think the story will be about. Ask them what clues the cover illustration gives to what the story will be about.

BUILD BACKGROUND Ask children to describe a typical Thanksgiving Day in their families. Discuss with children what their favorite dishes are. What do their families serve for dessert? Do they have many guests, or is it just their family members?

ELL Ask children to describe their first Thanksgiving Day. What did they eat? What were their favorite dishes? Do they have any day like Thanksgiving in their home countries?

PREVIEW/TAKE A PICTURE WALK Have children look at the illustrations. Ask how the illustrations give clues to what happens in the story. Have them look at the illustrations on pages 5 and 8. In which picture are guests arriving, and in which picture are they leaving? What clues in the pictures help children answer this question?

READ THE BOOK

SET PURPOSE Have children set a purpose for reading *Together for Thanksgiving*. Ask them to think about how their own families' celebrations compare to the one in the story.

STRATEGY SUPPORT: VISUALIZE Explain that writers use words to help a reader visualize, such as words that help us imagine how something looks, feels, tastes, smells, or sounds. Have children use a graphic organizer to note words that help them use each of their five senses.

COMPREHENSION QUESTIONS

PAGE 3 How do people travel to be with their families for Thanksgiving? *(by car and plane)*

PAGE 4 Where is the turkey cooking? *(in the oven)*

PAGE 6 The family and friends at the table give thanks before eating. If you were sitting with them, what would you be thankful for? *(Possible responses: my family, my dog, the food)*

PAGE 7 What happens after the meal but before they all play ball in the backyard? *(Everyone helps clean up.)*

PAGE 8 What kind of a day did everyone have? *(Everyone had fun.)*

PAGE 8 How do people feel about leaving at the end of the day? *(They are sorry to go.)*

REVIEW THE BOOK

THINK AND SHARE

1. Possible responses: They all enjoy Thanksgiving with family and friends. It says they all had fun. The illustrations show them having a good time.
2. Possible responses: saw people arriving, heard them saying hello, smelled dishes of food they brought
3. Possible responses: thanks, giving, sing, tank, than, sting
4. Aunt Amy brought stuffing; Uncle Ralph brought apple pie; Grandma brought sweet potatoes; Mary Jo brought green beans.

EXTEND UNDERSTANDING Ask children to consider what the *main idea* of this story is. Have them say it in one sentence.

RESPONSE OPTIONS

WRITING Have children visualize their Thanksgiving dinner spread out on a table in front of their family and them. Have children describe in a short paragraph who is at the table and the different types of food there. Make sure they describe the smells and tastes of all of the dishes.

SOCIAL STUDIES CONNECTION

Time For SOCIAL STUDIES

Have children research the history of Thanksgiving, using either the library or the Internet. What did the Pilgrims eat at their first Thanksgiving? What were they thankful for? What kind of things did they learn from the Native Americans?

Skill Work

TEACH/REVIEW VOCABULARY

Go over the meanings of the vocabulary words. Tell children you have chosen a mystery word and it is their job to guess what it is, based on three clues about the word. Create clues for all other vocabulary words.

ELL Have children write the vocabulary words on cards. Then ask them to look up the words in the dictionary and write the meanings on the backs of the cards. Finally, have them drill each other using the cards.

TARGET SKILL AND STRATEGY

DRAW CONCLUSIONS Remind children that *drawing conclusions* means thinking about the facts and details presented and deciding something about them. Have children look at the cover illustration. Ask them what they imagine the people on the cover are doing, and ask them to support their answers with clues from the illustration.

VISUALIZE Remind children that to *visualize* is to create a picture in your mind. While the term *visualize* seems to involve only the sense of sight, visualizing includes all of the senses (seeing, smelling, hearing, touching, and tasting) so that the reader becomes truly involved with the scene. Encourage children to look for words that help them visualize as they read this story.

ADDITIONAL SKILL INSTRUCTION

MAIN IDEA Remind children that we can tell the *main idea*, or what a story is all about, in one or two sentences. As they read, ask children to think about this story's main idea.

Name _____

Draw Conclusions

Think about the story *Together for Thanksgiving*. Then think about what you already know about Thanksgiving Day. Circle the phrase that best completes each conclusion below.

1. People go by car or plane to Thanksgiving dinner, so

   a. some live nearby and some live far away.

   b. everyone lives far away.

   c. they do not like to travel.

2. Everyone brings a dish, so

   a. there is not enough food.

   b. there is lots of food.

   c. there is no dessert.

3. Everyone helps clean up, so

   a. it gets done quickly.

   b. it takes a long time.

   c. they do not want to play.

4. What more do you know about Thanksgiving Day? Write your own conclusion on the line below.

_____

- -

_____

- -

_____

Name _____

Vocabulary

Choose the word from the box that best completes each sentence.
You may use one word more than once.

Words to Know

behind	brought	door	everybody
minute	promise	sorry	

1. John was _____ he couldn't come.

2. The guests knocked on the front _____ .

3. _____ ate some turkey.

4. My aunt _____ pumpkin pie.

5. We made a _____ to help clean up.

6. Dinner will be ready in a _____ .

7. Yummy smells came from _____ the kitchen door.

8. Dad _____ the turkey out on a large platter.

The Science Fair

SUMMARY This story follows a group of second-grade children as they build a model volcano and enter it in the school science fair. To their delight, the model erupts on cue, and the class wins the prize.

LESSON VOCABULARY

guess	pretty	science
shoe	village	watch
won		

INTRODUCE THE BOOK

INTRODUCE THE TITLE AND AUTHOR Discuss with children the title and the author of *The Science Fair*. Ask: What do you think will happen at the science fair?

BUILD BACKGROUND Ask children if they have ever attended or participated in a science fair. Find out if they have read about science fairs in the news. If not, ask them what kinds of science projects they might like to make to show other people. Spark discussion by offering such ideas as building a simple computer, designing a computer game, or making a model dinosaur skeleton. Explain that the purpose of a science fair is to show and teach others something interesting that you have learned.

PREVIEW/USE ILLUSTRATIONS Have children read the title and look carefully at the illustrations. Discuss what these suggest about the story's content and possible ending. Look, for example, at the illustration on page 4 and ask: What can you tell about these children by looking at this picture? After drawing their attention to the illustration on page 7, ask: Why do you think the judges are awarding a blue ribbon to these children?

READ THE BOOK

SET PURPOSE Guide children to set their own purposes for reading the selection. Children's interest in science, school fairs, or working together on some kind of group project should guide this purpose. Suggest that children imagine a scientific topic of interest to them.

STRATEGY SUPPORT: STORY STRUCTURE As children read, identifying the *story structure* helps them understand how one event leads logically to the next—in chronological sequence in this instance. This also helps them sort out the main ideas and events from the supporting details.

COMPREHENSION QUESTIONS

PAGE 5 Why did the children decide to build a model volcano for the science fair? *(They were studying volcanoes.)*

PAGE 6 What was the first thing the children did once they started to build their model volcano? *(They put an empty soda bottle on a baking sheet.)*

PAGES 6–7 What do you think the author wished to express about science fairs? *(They can be exciting.)*

PAGE 7 How did the children feel about winning the prize? How do you know? *(They were excited. The author used an exclamation point to convey excitement.)*

REVISIT THE BOOK

THINK AND SHARE

1. Possible response: to show children working together on a project that wins a prize
2. Possible response: 1. Class discusses fun ideas. 2. Class decides to build a volcano. 3. Class works together to build the volcano.
3. Possible response: Studying science helps us learn more about our world, so we can live safely and protect our environment too.
4. Possible response: Several children suggest ideas, and the class picks the project they want to do.

EXTEND UNDERSTANDING Explain to children that fictional stories often have *themes*, or big ideas, that convey a general truth or opinion. Help children find the theme of *The Science Fair*. After discussing the theme, ask them to use their own words to state it in a way that makes sense to them.

RESPONSE OPTIONS

WRITING Invite children to pick one topic they might like to explore for the purpose of entering a science fair. Ask them to write a few sentences describing why they like this topic and what they already know about it.

SCIENCE CONNECTION

Familiarize children with scientific procedure by having them perform a simple experiment and then record the results. They might, for example, compare the growth rate of two sunflowers, one in a southern window and one in a northern window.

Skill Work

TEACH/REVIEW VOCABULARY

Distribute simple written clues to each vocabulary word (such as *foot* for *shoe* or *town* for *village*) among children. Have a child read one clue, then ask a volunteer to identify the corresponding vocabulary word. Repeat with each vocabulary word.

ELL Invite children to draw picture clues for each vocabulary word on the board. Ask volunteers to name the word associated with the drawing.

TARGET SKILL AND STRATEGY

AUTHOR'S PURPOSE Remind children that an author has a reason or reasons for writing. Ask them if they think the author wants the story to be funny or to give us information. Have children look for any message or lesson the author may have for the readers. As children read, invite them to speculate about why the author wrote *The Science Fair*.

STORY STRUCTURE Remind children that the *structure* of a story is often a sequence from beginning to end, with one event leading to the next. Suggest that children make a simple story map as they read, noting the events in the order in which they happen. Point out, for example, that the children cannot enter the science fair until Miss Heath has announced the fair to the class.

ADDITIONAL SKILL INSTRUCTION

REALISM AND FANTASY Remind children that a *realistic story* tells something that could happen, while a *fantasy* is a story that could not happen. Ask children to discuss whether *The Science Fair* is a realistic story or a fantasy. Help them look for clues in the text and illustrations, such as the classroom setting and the fact that the characters are second-graders.

Name _____

Author's Purpose

Read the passage. Then answer the questions.

> We got an empty soda bottle. We molded dough around it. We filled the bottle with warm water and red food coloring. We added soap and baking soda.
>
> At the fair, we added vinegar to our volcano. It erupted perfectly. It looked like hot lava flowing down the sides. Guess who won first place? We did!

I. Why do you think the author wrote the first paragraph?

_____

_____

_____

2. Explain your answer.

_____

_____

_____

_____

_____

3. Why do you think the author wrote the second paragraph?

_____

_____

4. Explain your answer.

_____

_____

_____

_____

_____

Name _____

Vocabulary

Choose a word from the box to complete each sentence.

> ## Words to Know
>
> | guess | pretty | science | shoe |
> | village | watch | won | |

1. Miss Heath told her class that they would have a

   _____

   _____ fair.

   _____

   _____

2. Joe wanted to make a new kind of _____ .

   _____

   _____

3. The class worked _____ hard on their model.

   _____

   _____

4. Did you _____ the story's ending?

   _____

   _____

5. Many people from the _____ came to the fair.

   _____

   _____

6. They came to see who _____ .

   _____

   _____

7. Would you like to _____ a volcano erupt?

How Does the Mail Work?

SUMMARY This book explains the process of writing a letter, addressing the envelope, placing the stamp, mailing the letter, and having the letter transported to the recipient.

LESSON VOCABULARY

answer	company
faraway	parents
picture	school
wash	

INTRODUCE THE BOOK

INTRODUCE THE TITLE AND AUTHOR Discuss with the children the title and the author of *How Does the Mail Work?* Based on the title, ask children what kind of information they think this book will provide.

BUILD BACKGROUND Discuss what children know about mail, how to write a letter, and how the mail gets delivered. Ask if they have ever written or received a letter. Ask if they have ever mailed a letter. Have them talk about their experiences.

PREVIEW/TAKE A PICTURE WALK Invite children to look at the pictures in the selection. Start with the photograph on the title page. Ask children what they think this story will be about. Ask them to say what they think they will learn. What would they like to learn about the mail?

READ THE BOOK

SET PURPOSE Have children set a purpose for reading *How Does the Mail Work?* Children's interest in sending and receiving mail should guide this purpose. Suggest that children think of someone to whom they can write and plan to write a letter. You may wish to give them practice with the process by first "sending" a letter to a classmate.

STRATEGY SUPPORT: VISUALIZE As children read the selection, have them picture what is happening or visualize it in their minds. Visualizing gives them a chance to combine what they already know about how the mail works with new details. It also helps them to draw further conclusions about how the mail is delivered.

COMPREHENSION QUESTIONS

PAGE 3 What does the girl write about in her letter? *(herself, her school, her parents, her dog)*

PAGE 4 What does she write on the envelope? *(her aunt's address)*

PAGE 5 What does she stick on the envelope? *(a stamp)*

PAGE 6 Who goes with her to the mailbox? *(her dog)*

PAGE 7 Who takes the mail from the mailbox? *(the mail carrier)*

PAGE 8 What is her aunt's reaction when she gets the letter? *(She's happy.)*

REVISIT THE BOOK

THINK AND SHARE

1. Possible responses: I might like working outside and making people happy; I might not like working in the cold or meeting unfriendly dogs.
2. The mailing address is in the middle of the envelope. The stamp is in the upper right-hand corner.
3. *letter, address, envelope, stamp*
4. Answers will vary.

EXTEND UNDERSTANDING Have children look at the photograph on the title page. Invite them to read the address and say what the different parts of the address (name, street, city or town, state, zip code) stand for. Ask children to discuss in pairs the sequence of events that will happen after the girl mails the letter until it gets to the person it is intended for.

RESPONSE OPTIONS

WRITING Suggest that children write letters to family members who live with them. Provide them with envelopes and help them to write their addresses correctly. Make an exhibit of their letters and envelopes for a short time before mailing them.

SOCIAL STUDIES CONNECTION

Time For
SOCIAL
STUDIES

Children can learn more about how the mail works by doing guided research on the Internet or at the library. Suggest they find out how mail is sorted once it gets to the post office.

Skill Work

TEACH/REVIEW VOCABULARY

To reinforce the meaning of *company*, read page 6. Discuss how the words and the picture on this page help explain the meaning of the word. Talk about the expression "to keep someone company." Ask them if they have heard the word used in another way (*having company, working in a company*). Continue in a similar fashion with the remaining vocabulary words.

ELL Have children make clue cards for the words by having them write a vocabulary word on the front of each index card and draw a picture illustrating that word on the back. Stack the cards with the picture sides up. Then have children take turns drawing cards and figuring out the words. Continue until all children have had an opportunity to answer.

TARGET SKILL AND STRATEGY

DRAW CONCLUSIONS Remind children that to *draw conclusions* is to think about facts and details and decide something about them to make sense of what we read. Invite children to read page 8. Ask them to draw a conclusion about how the weather affects the delivery of the mail.

VISUALIZE Remind children that to *visualize* is to create pictures in their minds. As children read, suggest that they look at how the author helps us visualize each step of the mail. Ask them to visualize the process of writing, mailing, and delivering a letter as you read the story to them.

ADDITIONAL SKILL INSTRUCTION

SEQUENCE Remind children that the *sequence* is the order of events in a story. Sequence may also involve steps, as in mailing a letter. Children may want to list the steps of writing, addressing, sending, and receiving a letter to help them remember the sequence and visualize the process.

Name _____

Draw Conclusions

On the left are facts and details. On the right are decisions that could be made.

Draw a line to match each conclusion with the facts and details that support it.

Facts and Details

1. Maya wrote an address and put a stamp on an envelope.

2. Maya's dog was playing in the mud.

3. Maya and her dog walk to the mailbox.

4. Workers at the post office sort the mail.

Conclusions

a. Maya's dog needs a wash.

b. Maya is going to mail her letter.

c. Maya wrote a letter.

d. The mail is ready to be sent to all parts of the country.

5. Read the sentences below.
   Write a sentence to tell what you decide.

   Mail carriers deliver mail even if it's snowing or cold.
   It is snowing today.

Conclusion:

_____

- -

_____

- -

_____

58

Name _____

Vocabulary

Write the letters needed to complete each vocabulary word.

Words to Know
answer   company   faraway   parents
picture   school   wash

1. an _____

2. com _____

3. far _____

4. par _____

5. pic _____

6. w _____

7. sch _____

8. Draw a picture to show one of the words.

Write a sentence about your picture.

_____

_____

Casting Nets

SUMMARY How do people and spiders catch their food? The author invites readers to make many connections among facts and ideas. Interesting photographs support readers' comprehension of the descriptive text.

LESSON VOCABULARY

been	believe
caught	finally
today	tomorrow
whatever	

INTRODUCE THE BOOK

INTRODUCE THE TITLE AND AUTHOR Discuss with children the title and the author of *Casting Nets*. Ask children to comment on how the cover photograph relates to the title. Help children recognize how the topic relates to social studies.

BUILD BACKGROUND Ask children what they know about how people catch fish. Some children may have had experiences using a fishing rod or net. Others may have had experiences with butterfly nets. Encourage children to make generalizations about different types of nets and their shared purposes.

ELL Develop vocabulary and build background by creating word webs based on the topics discussed in the books. Have children brainstorm words that relate to fishing and spiders. After writing each word on a card, create word webs on a wall in the classroom. Allow children to guide the placement of the word cards in the webs.

PREVIEW/TAKE A PICTURE WALK Prompt children to scan the book and comment on the text features. Guide children to recognize that the author is comparing fishnets to spider webs by looking at the photographs.

READ THE BOOK

SET PURPOSE Children can set a purpose by first thinking about people who cast nets. Ask: Do you know of any animals that cast some sort of net? Have them write down one question they have about nets, fishermen, or spiders. Remind them to look for the answer to their questions as they read.

STRATEGY SUPPORT: MONITOR AND FIX UP As children read, remind them to draw upon their prior knowledge to check their understanding of the text. Ask: Are any facts from the text like or different from what you already know about fishing, nets, webs, and spiders? Which do you think are correct—information that you remember, or facts from the text? Encourage children who are not sure which information is correct to reread the text and look at the pictures. Suggest that children read slowly to improve their comprehension.

COMPREHENSION QUESTIONS

PAGE 4 What word means the same as the word *cast*? *(Possible response: throw)*

PAGE 6 How are fishing nets and spider webs different? *(Fishing nets are much bigger.)*

PAGE 7 Where does the spider's thread come from? *(The spider makes the silk thread inside its body.)*

PAGE 8 Why do bugs fly into the spider's web? *(Possible response: The web is hard to see.)*

REVISIT THE BOOK

THINK AND SHARE

1. Possible responses: The fish swim into the nets; the fishermen pull up the nets and scoop the fish out of the water.
2. Possible responses should show children's understanding of how to monitor and fix up while reading.
3. *fishermen, whatever, something;* additional compound words will vary.
4. Possible response: A spider's web looks like a net, and it is used to catch food.

EXTEND UNDERSTANDING Pause at page 5 and prompt children to make inferences from reading the text and looking at the photograph. Ask: Are fishermen the only people who eat the fish they catch? Why do you think they will be back tomorrow? If you eat fish, do you think the fish that you eat is caught in the same way? Are you surprised by all the fish sold at the market?

RESPONSE OPTIONS

WRITING Have children write acrostic poems using one of the shorter words in the book such as *fish, net, spin,* or *web.* They should write the word vertically with the first letters on each line spelling out the word they chose. Each line of their poems should start with a letter of their chosen words. Have dictionaries available for children to look up words to use in their poems.

SOCIAL STUDIES CONNECTION

Time For
SOCIAL
STUDIES

Arrange to have books in the classroom about similar topics, such as coastal Native American groups, whaling, marine life, and food chains. Have children give short reports to the class that compare *Casting Nets* to other books of their choice.

Skill Work

TEACH/REVIEW VOCABULARY

Reinforce the meanings of the vocabulary words by having children group them into the categories, *time* and *action.* Have each child write a sentence using one word from each category. Allow time for children to share their sentences with the class. Since the words *whatever* and *been* do not fit in either group, discuss these words separately and have children use them in sentences to show the meanings.

TARGET SKILL AND STRATEGY

CAUSE AND EFFECT Practice recognizing *cause-and-effect* relationships that are not signaled by clue words such as *because.* After page 5, ask: Why will many fishermen go back tomorrow? *(They need to catch more fish to eat or sell.)* Clarify the skill by prompting children to use the word *because* in their answers to connect the cause and effect.

MONITOR AND FIX UP Remind children to *monitor,* or check, their understanding of the text as they read. Tell children that they can *fix up* their understanding by changing the pace at which they read. Encourage children to take time to look at the photographs and captions. Ask children to explain how the photograph on page 8 helps them understand that a spider makes a web to catch its food. Then have children state the relationship between a spider and its web in their own words.

ADDITIONAL SKILL INSTRUCTION

COMPARE AND CONTRAST Remind children that when you *compare* two or more things, you show how they are alike and different. When you *contrast* two or more things, you show only how they are different. Familiarize children with clue words, such as *like, as, also, but,* and *unlike.* The author asks the reader to compare fishing nets to spider webs on page 6. Have children share their answers to the author's question.

Name _____

Cause and Effect

Draw a line to match each **cause** with its **effect**.

Causes

1. The spider is hungry.

2. A spider spins a sticky web.

3. There is a two-day storm.

4. Fishermen cast nets into the sea.

Effects

a. The fishermen have no fish to sell.

b. Fish are caught in the nets.

c. The spider eats a moth for dinner.

d. The moth is caught in the web.

5. Write a sentence that shows a cause and an effect. Use the clue word *because.*

_____
_____
_____
_____
_____

Name _____

Vocabulary

Draw a line to match the word with its meaning.

Words to Know
been   believe   caught   finally
today   tomorrow   whatever

1. been

2. believe

3. caught

4. finally

5. today

6. tomorrow

7. whatever

a. the next day

b. at the end

c. anything

d. to feel that something is true

e. this day

f. to have stayed or continued

g. grabbed hold of something

8. Write a sentence using *finally* and *whatever*.

_____

_____

_____

_____

Shy Ana

SUMMARY In *Shy Ana*, a young girl begins to overcome her shyness when she gets the idea to help her father shop at the market. It supports the lesson concept of when a creative idea can be a solution.

LESSON VOCABULARY

alone	buy
daughters	half
many	their
youngest	

INTRODUCE THE BOOK

INTRODUCE THE TITLE AND AUTHOR Discuss with children the title and the author of *Shy Ana*. Ask: What does the title and cover picture tell you about Ana?

BUILD BACKGROUND Ask children to discuss what it means to be shy. Have them share any situations in which they felt shy. Ask: Did your shyness make the situation more difficult? What did you do about it?

PREVIEW/TAKE A PICTURE WALK Have children look at the pictures in the book before reading. Ask: What do you think this story is about? Have children read the heading and view the photograph on page 12. Ask and discuss: Is this part of the story? What do you think this part of the book will tell us?

READ THE BOOK

SET PURPOSE Have children set a purpose for reading *Shy Ana*. You may need to work with children to have them set their own purposes. Ask: What do you want to know about Ana and what happens to her?

STRATEGY SUPPORT: PREDICT Remind children that as they read, they should think about what will probably happen next. They should look for clues that help *predict* what might happen next. Have them think about what they might do next if they were in the characters' places. After page 4, model: "What have I just read about? Ana is shy, and Mama needs help. What do I think will happen next? Ana will want to be alone. Why? Ana is shy, and I know that shy people like to be alone. Also, the picture shows Ana going in another direction." Have children record their predictions in graphic organizers. Have them give reasons to support their predictions, and revisit their predictions to see if they are correct or need to be revised.

COMPREHENSION QUESTIONS

PAGE 3 What happened at the beginning of the story? (*Possible response: On Papa's birthday, Mama wanted a family picture, but Ana wanted to be alone.*)

PAGES 6–7 Why didn't Clara let Papa rest? (*Possible response: There was no one else who could get the tortillas.*)

PAGE 10 Why were the farmers at the market so nice? (*Possible response: They wanted to please their customers.*)

PAGE 11 What did you learn about people by reading about Ana? (*Possible response: With help, shy people can stop being shy.*)

PAGE 11 Write your own title for this story. Your title should tell what the story is all about. (*Possible response: Ana Stops Being Shy.*)

REVISIT THE BOOK

THINK AND SHARE

1. Possible response: People can overcome shyness in the right situation.
2. The clue is when Ana tells her father that she wants to help. I predict that she will be less shy at the market.
3. Possible response: Ana thinks she is too young to help.
4. Possible response: The farmers there were very nice.

EXTEND UNDERSTANDING Have children analyze the story's setting. Remind children that a story's setting is where and when the story takes place. Ask: Where did most of the story happen? Where else did it take place?

RESPONSE OPTIONS

VIEWING Have children describe what is happening in each picture in the story.

ART CONNECTION

Invite children to draw a picture of a situation in which they might feel shy. Have them write a caption for the picture that gives a possible solution for overcoming their shyness.

Skill Work

TEACH/REVIEW VOCABULARY

Have children make sets of vocabulary word cards. Write these phrases on the board: *belongs to them, a lot, by myself, pay for, one of two parts, lowest in age, girl children.* Read each phrase aloud. Ask children to show the vocabulary word that best matches each phrase.

TARGET SKILL AND STRATEGY

THEME AND PLOT Explain that every story has one big idea. After children finish reading, ask: What did you learn from this story about all people, not just Ana? (*People can overcome shyness.*) Remind children that the plot is what happens in the beginning, middle, and end of the story. After page 5, write on the board: *Ana stayed out of the way when Mama looked for Clara and Ana. Mama took a picture. Clara asks Papa to get more tortillas. Ana wants to help and doesn't feel shy.* Say: Place these events in order from first to last.

ELL Help children complete a simple sequence diagram to plot what happens in the beginning, middle, and end of the story.

PREDICT Tell children to think about, or *predict,* what will probably happen next. Have children pause after reading page 9 and predict what will happen next. Remind them to check their predictions to see if they were correct.

ADDITIONAL SKILL INSTRUCTION

MAIN IDEA Remind children that, as they read, they should ask: What is the story all about? After page 10, write on the board: *The farmers are nice. Ana doesn't feel shy at all! Ana gets just what Mama asked for. Going home with Papa, she feels happy.* Ask: What is this page all about? Point out to children that the second sentence is what the page is all about.

Name _____

Theme and Plot

Write the answer to each question.

1. How did Ana act at the beginning of the story?

   _____

   -

   _____

2. What did Ana do in the middle of the story?

   _____

   -

   _____

3. How did Ana act at the end of the story?

   _____

   -

   _____

4. How did Ana change?

   _____

   -

   _____

   -

   _____

5. What is the "big idea" of this story?

   _____

   -

   _____

   -

   _____

Name _____

Vocabulary

Write a word from the box that means the same as the phrase.

Words to Know
alone buy daughters half
many their youngest

1. more than a few

_____

2. all by myself

_____

3. one of two parts

_____

4. daddy's girls

_____

5. belonging to them

_____

6. baby of the bunch

_____

7. pay money to get

_____

An Orange Floats

SUMMARY This book explains the scientific method through describing an experiment about water and flotation. By providing an example of how a scientific hypothesis is formed, it supports the lesson concept of where new ideas come from.

LESSON VOCABULARY

clothes	hours
money	neighbor
only	question
taught	

INTRODUCE THE BOOK

INTRODUCE THE TITLE AND AUTHOR Discuss with children the title and the author of *An Orange Floats.* Say: "Look at the cover. How does the book's title relate to the cover illustration? What other ideas might be discussed in the selection? Scientists test new ideas. How might this book have something to do with science?"

BUILD BACKGROUND Ask children to share what they know about things that float. Ask: Have you ever floated in water? Have you ever seen objects floating in water? Where? Have children discuss their experiences.

PREVIEW/TAKE A PICTURE WALK Have children look at the pictures in the book before reading. Ask: What do you think the girl is doing? What do you think this book is about?

READ THE BOOK

SET PURPOSE Have children set a purpose for reading *An Orange Floats.* Remind children of what they discussed in the introduction. You may need to work with children to have them set their own purposes.

STRATEGY SUPPORT: MONITOR AND FIX UP Remind children that good readers know that what they read must make sense. Tell children that they should check as they read this book to make sure they understand what they are reading. Explain that they can *skim* and *scan* to help their understanding. Skimming is looking quickly through the book to see what it is about. Scanning is looking quickly through the words and pictures to find information you may have missed or information ahead in the book that may help you. Have children read the text on page 6, then model: "Does this make sense? Do boats and birds only float on salty water? Oh, when I scan page 7, I see that they float on fresh water too." Encourage children to glance through the text whenever they have trouble understanding this book.

ELL Have children use a steps-in-a-process chart to keep track of the steps of the experiment that is described in the book.

COMPREHENSION QUESTIONS

PAGES 4–5 Do heavy things always sink? How do you know? *(Possible answer: No, I know that heavy things, like boats, can float.)*

PAGE 6 Why does a scientist do a test? *(to find out the answer to a question)*

PAGE 9 Why should you use the same orange? *(to make sure that the salt, not a different orange, affects the results)*

REVIST THE BOOK

THINK AND SHARE

1. Salt was added to the water; the orange floated.
2. The text says that scientists think up questions about what they want to know.
3. Responses will vary, but should include the concept of learning by investigating answers to questions.
4. Possible responses: 1. Give a hypothesis. 2. Test your guess. 3. Collect data. 4. Make and share your conclusion.

EXTEND UNDERSTANDING Point out the chart on page 5. Ask: Why does the book show us this chart? Guide children to see how it helps us understand how to form a scientific question.

RESPONSE OPTIONS

WRITING Have children write two or three sentences that summarize the test results in the book.

SCIENCE CONNECTION

Have children work in pairs to design an experiment to see whether an orange will float the same in fresh water as in other kinds of water, such as muddy water, colored water, or hot water. Encourage children to do the experiment at home with an adult and to share the results in class.

Skill Work

TEACH/REVIEW VOCABULARY

Have children make sets of vocabulary word cards. Then read these clues and have children show the correct word: *It's bigger than minutes. This needs an answer. The teacher did this. It's one of a kind. Use this to buy things. You wear these. This person lives next door.*

TARGET SKILL AND STRATEGY

CAUSE AND EFFECT Remind children as they read to think about things that happen *(effects)* and why those things happen *(causes)*. Think aloud: "Because I was hungry, I ate. What happened is, 'I ate.' Why it happened is 'I was hungry.'" Remind children to look for clue words such as *because, so, if, then,* and *since.* Model questions to ask after page 4, "What happened? Clothes float, then sink. Why did it happen? They get wetter." Have children use a cause-and-effect chart to keep track of what happened and why it happened as they read the book.

MONITOR AND FIX UP Tell children that they should *monitor* as they read to make sure they understand the text. Explain that they can skim and scan to *fix up* their understanding. After page 3, have children scan ahead through page 6 to find out what the sentence *Scientists do a lot of wondering* means. Remind children that checking their understanding and skimming and scanning as they read will make it easier to understand what happened and why it happened.

ADDITIONAL SKILL INSTRUCTION

DRAW CONCLUSIONS Tell children that they should use what they have read and seen and what they know about real life to *draw conclusions,* or figure out more about what happens in the book. After page 10, ask: Did the girl follow the directions exactly? How do you know? *(No, I can see that the orange in the picture is peeled. Now she is pouring water. She should have done that first.)*

Name _____

Cause and Effect

Fill in the numbered boxes to tell what happened or why it happened.

Why did it happen? (Cause)	What happened? (Effect)

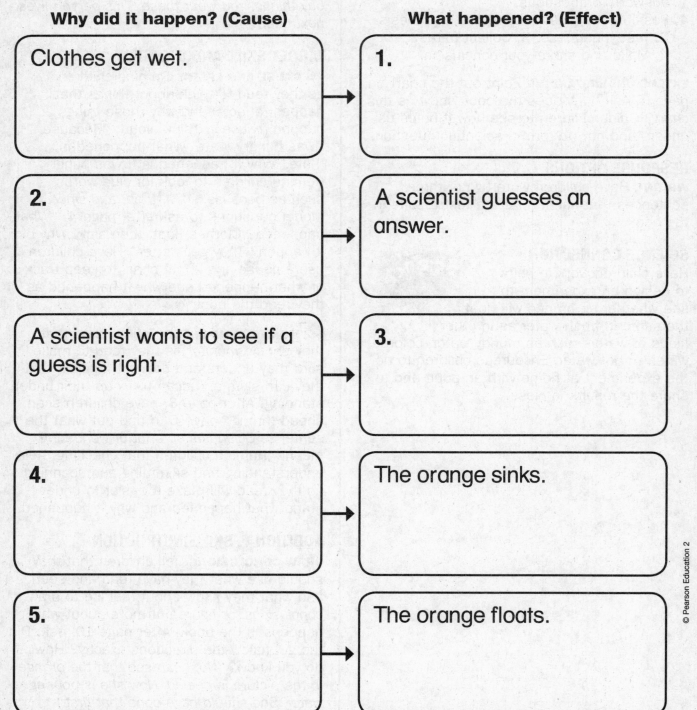

Clothes get wet.

1.

2.

A scientist guesses an answer.

A scientist wants to see if a guess is right.

3.

4.

The orange sinks.

5.

The orange floats.

© Pearson Education 2

70

Name _____

Vocabulary

Write the word from the box that goes with each picture.

Words to Know
clothes   hours   money   neighbor   only   question   taught

1. _____

3. _____

2. _____

4. _____

5. Write the words from the box that have more than one syllable.

_____

_____

_____

_____

The Butterfly Quilt

SUMMARY This fictional text describes a girl's visit to her grandmother's house and the story of her family's "Butterfly Quilt."

LESSON VOCABULARY

blankets	pretended
quilt	stuffing
trunks	unpacked
wrapped	

INTRODUCE THE BOOK

INTRODUCE THE TITLE AND AUTHOR Discuss with children the title and author of *The Butterfly Quilt*. Ask: Who do you see on the cover? How do you think these people are related? What do you think we will learn about the butterfly quilt we see on the cover? Turn to the title page. Ask: What do you see here? How do you think these things relate to what we see on the cover?

BUILD BACKGROUND Invite children to share family stories and memories. Ask: Does your family have any special things that have been passed down from generation to generation? Why has your family kept these things? What makes them special to your family? Why should we remember these things and the stories that go with them? Why are family stories important?

PREVIEW/TAKE A PICTURE WALK Preview the book with the children, looking at the illustrations. Have children describe what they see happening on the page and what they think this book might be about. Call special attention to the different colors and patterns of the fabrics in the quilt on pages 8 and 9.

READ THE BOOK

SET PURPOSE Based on your discussion of the cover of the book, ask children what they would like to learn about these characters. Ask: What do you think the "butterfly quilt" is? It looks to me like the butterfly quilt is important to this family and I'd like to read to find out why.

STRATEGY SUPPORT: STORY STRUCTURE Have children take notes as they read and then refer to these notes in order to retell the story after reading. Encourage them to use signal words such as *first, then, next,* and *last* as they describe the sequence of events.

COMPREHENSION QUESTIONS

PAGE 3 Using the picture on page 3, compare and contrast the mother and grandmother. How are they alike and how are they different? (*Possible response: Both are women, wearing earrings. One has gray hair, one has brown hair; one is wearing a dress, one is wearing a shirt and pants.*)

PAGE 5 What can you tell about the grandmother? (*She is helpful and likes sharing about her family and the quilt.*)

PAGE 7 Why do you think it took such a long time for Nell to finish the quilt. (*Possible response: It took a long time to collect fabric, and there were many different steps to putting together the quilt.*)

PAGE 9 Why do you think Nana and the girl enjoy looking at the different fabrics in the quilt? (*because they are from many different family members*)

PAGE 11 Why is it important to the girl to create another story quilt? (*To share her family's story and save it for future generations*)

REVISIT THE BOOK

READER RESPONSE

1. Both are special, made by families to pass down, made of repeating patterns; one has a butterfly pattern, the other has diamond shapes and stars.

2. Saved old clothing, made butterfly wings out of the cloth, sewed wings on squares, sewed them together

3. Box, chest, container

4. Possible response: maybe she could not afford it, or maybe she wanted to remember the people to whom the cloth belonged.

EXTEND UNDERSTANDING Remind children that "setting" is where a story takes place. Ask: Where does this story take place? If the book didn't tell us on page 3 that the girl and Mama are visiting Nana, what other clues from the book would help tell us where the story takes place?

RESPONSE OPTIONS

SPEAKING Encourage children to ask family members about stories from their family's past. Children can prepare and share these stories with the group. If available, they may also bring and/or describe a special item that connects to the story.

ART CONNECTION

Provide children with a variety of brightly colored construction paper, tissue paper, and wrapping paper. Provide each child with a butterfly-shaped template to create and decorate his or her own "butterfly square." Put these all on a bulletin board to create a class "butterfly quilt." Look at and discuss the squares, making sure to point out the similarities and differences between butterflies as well as who made each one.

Skill Work

TEACH/REVIEW VOCABULARY

To aid comprehension, help children locate each of the vocabulary words in the book. Read the words in context on pages 4 and 5 and discuss what is happening in the story.

ELL Use visual clues, such as the illustrations and even pantomime, to help children understand the meanings of the vocabulary words.

TARGET SKILL AND STRATEGY

COMPARE AND CONTRAST Explain to children that to compare and contrast means to describe how things are alike and different. Turn to pages 8 and 9 and guide children in comparing and contrasting the fabrics they see pictured. Encourage them to describe the colors, patterns, and shapes of the butterflies. Ask: How are each of these butterflies the same? How are they different? Which butterflies are most similar to each other? Which ones are most different?

TEXT STRUCTURE As children read, help them keep track of the order of events by writing notes or using a simple diagram. As you continue through the text, use signal words to assist children. Ask: What happened first? Then what did the girl do? What do you think will happen next?

ADDITIONAL SKILL INSTRUCTION

CHARACTER Remind children that a character is a person in a story. Ask them to describe what they know about the girl based on the information in the story. Encourage children to make higher-order conclusions about the girl. These may include: she is creative (plays dress-up), is interested in her family's history, shows thoughtfulness about her family and the future (wants to create another special quilt).

Name _____

Compare and Contrast

In *The Butterfly Quilt*, you learned how this special blanket helps preserve family memories. Compare and contrast how quilts and photographs can each help preserve memories. Use the Venn diagram to organize your ideas.

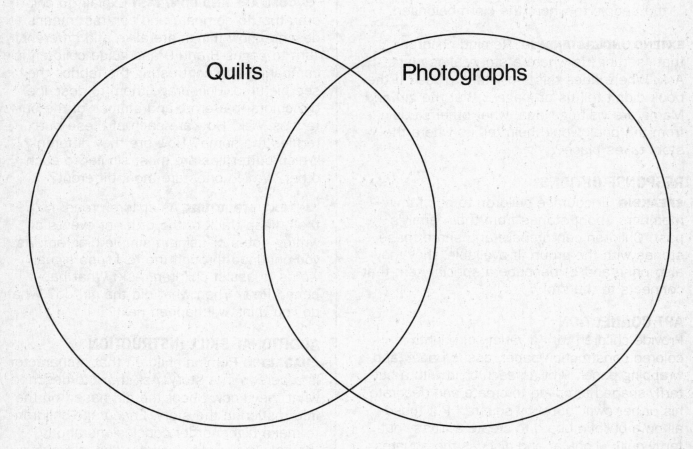

Name _____

Vocabulary

For each sentence, write the correct word in the space provided.

1. Quilts and old clothes are sometimes stored in _____.
   stuffing   trunks   blankets

2. I _____ myself in a quilt to keep warm.
   unpacked   pretended   wrapped

3. Quilts are like _____.
   trunks   blankets   stuffing

4. A quilt is filled with _____ to make it thick.
   stuffing   trunks   quilt

5. A _____ is a special way to keep memories.
   trunks   quilt   blankets

6. I _____ the quilt from the trunk.
   wrapped   pretended   unpacked

7. I played dress-up and _____ that I
   lived a long time ago.
   pretended   wrapped   stuffing

Grow a Tomato!

SUMMARY This informational text describes how to grow, care for, and harvest tomato plants.

LESSON VOCABULARY

bumpy	fruit
harvest	roots
smooth	soil
vines	

INTRODUCE THE BOOK

INTRODUCE THE TITLE AND AUTHOR Discuss with children the title and the author of *Grow a Tomato!* Have the children describe the cover illustration and share what they think this book might be about. Ask: What do you think you might learn from this book?

BUILD BACKGROUND Engage the children in a discussion of plants. Ask: Have any of you ever grown a plant? What was it? How did you care for it? What do plants need to grow?

PREVIEW/TAKE A PICTURE WALK Invite the children to preview the book, looking at the pictures. Encourage them to discuss the illustrations and make predictions about the text. Draw attention to the call-outs on page 11 and discuss how this information can help them understand the text. Ask: Why do you think the author included these call-outs? What information do they contain?

ELL Invite English language learners to share the call-out words on page 11 in their native languages.

READ THE BOOK

SET PURPOSE Guide the children in determining a purpose for reading. Based on your discussion of the title, elicit from children that this will probably be an instructional text with information on how to do something. Ask: Why would someone want to read this book? How do you think we will be able to use the information in this book?

STRATEGY SUPPORT: ASK QUESTIONS After reading, encourage children to ask questions about the text. Remind them that asking questions can help them better understand what they have read. Write questions down that can be answered using the text. Give each child (or pair of children) one question and have them find the answers to their questions in the text. Share these with the others. Children should say the page number and also read the sentence or sentences where they found their answers.

COMPREHENSION QUESTIONS

PAGE 3 This page says it is good to grow your vegetables. Is this a statement of fact or opinion, and why? *(Opinion. "Good" can't be proved true or false.)*

PAGES 4-5 At this point, you've learned a little about how to start growing tomato plants. Think of some questions that the book might help you answer as you continue reading. *(Possible responses: What are the next steps? What else will I learn about growing a tomato plant?)*

PAGE 7 What are the topic and main idea on page 7? *(Topic: fertilizer. Main idea: fertilizer helps plants grow.)*

PAGE 10 Why do you think you need to keep the plants healthy and green? *(So they won't die and will grow good tomatoes.)*

REVISIT THE BOOK

READER RESPONSE

1. fact; *need*
2. Answers should reflect that children know the basic steps in growing plants. Questions should reflect more specific information that is needed, such as size, placement, etc.
3. Possible responses: *soft, hard, dry, wet, rough*
4. Attaching tomato vines (stems of the plant) to stakes (wooden poles) keeps the tomatoes off the ground.

EXTEND UNDERSTANDING Look again at the illustrations in the book. Now that children have finished reading, encourage them to describe how the illustrations help support the text and aid comprehension. Point out that when they previewed the book, the illustrations helped give them an idea what the text would be about. Ask: As you read, how did the illustrations help you better understand the words on the page? Was there any information you didn't understand at first and then were able to figure out by using the illustrations?

RESPONSE OPTIONS

SPEAKING Ask the children to describe the process of growing tomato plants, step by step. Encourage them to refer to the book to remember details and sequence.

SCIENCE CONNECTION

Using this book and others for reference, plant and grow tomatoes as a class. Keep them on a windowsill or in a greenhouse where the children can take turns caring for the tomatoes and monitoring their growth.

Skill Work

TEACH/REVIEW VOCABULARY

Have children write the vocabulary words on their own paper and draw a representation of each. Discuss the words and use them in context as children complete this activity.

TARGET SKILL AND STRATEGY

FACT AND OPINION Explain to children that a statement of fact is something that can be proved true or false. As you read page 8, guide the children in determining whether this information is a statement of fact or opinion. Say: This page says that I must do something to hold up the tomato vines; otherwise they will flop on the ground. Can this statement be proved true or false? What does that tell us about this statement?

ASK QUESTIONS As you preview the book and have children make predictions, model for them how to ask questions about the text. Say: I wonder how the author organized this book. What supplies do I need to grow a tomato plant? What are the steps in growing a tomato plant? I'm going to keep these questions in mind as I read and see if the book answers them for me.

ADDITIONAL SKILL INSTRUCTION

MAIN IDEA Model for the children how to determine the main idea. Read together the paragraph on page 6. Say: I think that the topic of this paragraph is watering your tomato plants. I decided that the main idea of the paragraph is that tomato plants need plenty of water because it says they are thirsty and not to let the soil stay dry for too long.

Name _____

Fact and Opinion

Read each sentence and think about if it is a statement of fact or a statement of opinion. Then circle your answer.

1. It is good to grow your own vegetables.

   Statement of fact   Statement of opinion

2. After planting tomato seeds, soon green stems will peek out and leaves will grow.

   Statement of fact   Statement of opinion

3. Tomato plants need care as they grow.

   Statement of fact   Statement of opinion

4. It is fun to grow tomato plants.

   Statement of fact   Statement of opinion

5. Tomato plants can grow quite tall.

   Statement of fact   Statement of opinion

Name _____

Vocabulary

Choose words from the Word Box to complete the sentences

> bumpy   fruit   harvest   roots   smooth   soil   vines

To grow a tomato plant, first, plant seeds in small pots. Put the pots in a sunny place. Soon green stems and leaves will grow. After six weeks, bring the pots outside and dig holes in the soil.

1. Take rocks out of the soil so that it will not be _____ .

2. Be careful not to break the _____ when you slide the plants out of the pots.

3. Place the plants in the _____ and pat around them.

4. Water your plants and tie the _____ .

5. Soon flowers will bloom and _____ will appear.

6. When your plants are red, it is time for _____ .

7. Wash them so they are clean and _____ .

A Frog's Life

SUMMARY This book follows the stages of a frog's life. These stages include egg, tadpole, froglet, and full-grown frog.

LESSON VOCABULARY

crawls	insects
pond	powerful
shed	skin
wonderful	

INTRODUCE THE BOOK

INTRODUCE THE TITLE AND AUTHOR Discuss with children the title and author of *A Frog's Life*. Have them look at the cover. What do they think the book will be about? Do they think this will be a fiction or nonfiction book? What clues tell them this?

BUILD BACKGROUND Ask children to tell you what they know about frogs. If children are unaware that frogs go through various stages (egg, tadpole, froglet, frog), briefly discuss the stages before children begin to read.

PREVIEW/TAKE A PICTURE WALK Invite children to look at the photos in the book. Ask them to tell you how they think the photos might help them understand the information they will be reading. Point out the labels and the fact that they are used to name the different stages in a frog's life and show the different body parts. Then, show children the diagram on page 12 and make sure they understand that the arrows are showing the cycle of events.

READ THE BOOK

SET PURPOSE Have children set a purpose for reading *A Frog's Life*. Children's own interests should guide this purpose. Perhaps they want to learn how a tadpole is different from a full-grown frog or how many stages a frog goes through from egg to full-grown frog.

STRATEGY SUPPORT: GRAPHIC ORGANIZERS Remind children that people use graphic organizers to help them understand and remember information. Review with children the three-column chart on the last page and look at the diagram on page 12. Let them know that this diagram shows the stages in a frog's life, and they should look at it when they fill out the chart. Tell children that they should also use the photos in the book as well as written information to give them more details to use in the chart.

COMPREHENSION QUESTIONS

PAGE 6 What do tadpoles look like when they first hatch? *(like little fish)*

PAGE 9 What happens after a tadpole loses its tail? *(it crawls on to land and becomes a froglet.)*

PAGE 12 Look at the diagram. Which does a froglet look more like, a tadpole or a frog? *(frog)*

REVISIT THE BOOK

READER RESPONSE

1. The tadpole has a tail; the frog does not. The frog has a larger body. Both the tadpole and the frog have four legs.
2. Tadpole: swims, gills, no legs. Froglet: crawls on land, lungs, loses tail, four legs. Frog: crawls on land, lungs, no tail, four legs.
3. To drop something off. *Shed* also means a small house to put tools in.
4. Responses will vary.

EXTEND UNDERSTANDING Ask children if they looked at the photographs and labels before reading the information on each page, during reading, or after reading. Discuss how the photos and labels helped them to better understand what they were learning about frogs.

RESPONSE OPTIONS

WRITING Have children pick one of the stages of the frog's life. Using the information in the book, children should draw and label their chosen stage. Under the picture, they can write a few sentences about what they have drawn.

SCIENCE CONNECTION

TIME FOR Science

There are many different species of frogs. Display a variety of books about frogs and invite children to explore the information about what the frogs look like and what their habitats are.

Skill Work

TEACH/REVIEW VOCABULARY

Write each of the vocabulary words on index cards. Put the cards face down. Then have each child pick a card and use his or her word in sentences that give clues to the word's meaning. Example: We like to swim in a pond.

ELL Some of the vocabulary words can have more than one meaning. Help ELL children to understand that in the context of this story *powerful* means "strong," and *shed* means to "get rid of."

TARGET SKILL AND STRATEGY

COMPARE AND CONTRAST Remind children that to compare and contrast things means to look for how things are alike or different. As children read, ask them to pay special attention to how the frog's body changes in each stage of its life.

GRAPHIC ORGANIZERS Discuss why people use graphic organizers. (To help them organize and remember information.) Point out the three-column chart on the last page of the book. Ask children to tell you how the chart might help them see how the different stages in a frog's life are alike and how they are different. Let them know they will be filling out the chart after reading the book.

ADDITIONAL SKILL INSTRUCTION

SEQUENCE Tell children that as they read *A Frog's Life*, they should think about what happens first, next, and last. After reading *A Frog's Life*, have the children tell you about the different stages that a frog goes through and what happens, or the events, in each stage. To help them remember the stages, they can look at the diagram on page 12. Children do not need to tell you the stages in order. Write down what they say. Then, read back the events and discuss whether or not they make sense and if they follow the actual order of what happens in a frog's life. Then, work as a group to reorder the events in the proper order.

Name _____

COMPARE and CONTRAST

1. Circle the picture of a tadpole.
Then draw a line to the kind of food it eats.

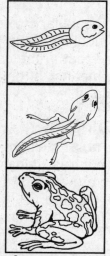 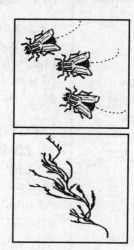

2. Circle the picture of a frog.
Then draw a line to the kind of food it eats.

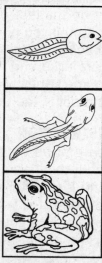 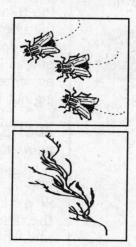

3. Circle the animal that most looks like a tiny fish.

Frog   **Froglet**   **Tadpole**

4. Circle the animal that lays eggs.

Frog   **Froglet**   **Tadpole**

Name _____

Vocabulary

Words to Know
crawls   insects   pond   powerful skin   shed   wonderful

Write a word from the box that has the same meaning as the phrase.

1. lose outer skin layer   _____

2. covering for your body   _____

3. very strong   _____

4. exciting and great   _____

5. **Choose** a vocabulary word to finish each sentence.

_____

A. The baby _____ across the floor.

B. Frogs like to eat _____.

C. We swim in the _____.

A Big Change

SUMMARY A young girl is sad when her family moves from the city to the country, but she soon finds reasons to like her new home.

LESSON VOCABULARY

block	chuckle
fair	giant
strong	tears
trouble	

INTRODUCE THE BOOK

INTRODUCE THE TITLE AND AUTHOR Discuss with children the title and author of *A Big Change*. Ask children who the people on the cover of the book might be. Based on the title, what might happen to those people?

BUILD BACKGROUND Invite children to compare any knowledge of city life with knowledge of country life. Which setting would they prefer to live in and why?

PREVIEW Have children preview the book. Tell them to pay attention to the expressions on the characters' faces. What do children think is happening in the story and how might the characters be feeling?

READ THE BOOK

SET PURPOSE Have children set a purpose for reading *A Big Change*. Children might want to find out what happens to the family and how the big change affects them.

STRATEGY SUPPORT: SUMMARIZE In order to help children practice summarizing, discuss a class trip or some other special experience that the class has shared. Help children to recap only the most important things, or the main ideas, about what happened. When you feel they understand how to express the main idea of what happened, have them read the story. Remind them that as they read *A Big Change*, they should take time to stop and think about the main things that are happening.

COMPREHENSION QUESTIONS

PAGES 3–5 How does Jen feel about leaving the city? *(really sad)*

PAGES 6–7 Could the things you read about on these pages really happen? *(yes)*

PAGE 9 What important information is in the picture that is not in what you read? Does it give you a hint of what might happen next? *(The goats are for sale. Possible response: Yes, Jen might get a goat.)*

PAGE 11 Were you surprised that Jen ended up liking the country? Why or why not? *(Responses will vary.)*

REVISIT THE BOOK

READER RESPONSE

1. Jen is sad about leaving the city. Her family moves to the country. Jen gets a goat and goes fishing. She decides she likes the country.
2. City: Jen missed her friend Lisa, her neighborhood, the park, her school, and her pigeon. Country: Jen likes her new goat and going fishing.
3. A laugh
4. Possible response: She's not ready to think of the place as home. She's still sad about leaving the city.

EXTEND UNDERSTANDING This is a realistic story because everything in the story could really have happened. Discuss ways that this story could be turned into a fantasy. For example, what if the pigeon at the beginning talked to Jen. Or, what if Jen had discovered a tree in the country that grew apples made of gold. Encourage children to think of ways to turn the story into a fantasy while still keeping the same characters and theme. (Moving from one place to another can be hard, but you might really like where you end up.)

RESPONSE OPTIONS

WRITING/ VISUAL Encourage children to draw pictures about anywhere they would like to live. Under the picture they can write a few sentences about why they want to live there.

SOCIAL STUDIES CONNECTION

Time For
SOCIAL
STUDIES

Display books about different cities and different rural areas. After children look at the books, encourage them to discuss what they thought was most interesting about each place.

Skill Work

TEACH/REVIEW VOCABULARY

Write the following words on the board: *bubble, buckle, care, long, clock, hears.* Challenge children to choose a vocabulary word that rhymes with each of the words on the board. Then ask them which of the vocabulary words does not rhyme with any of the words on the board *(giant).*

ELL Check children's understanding of vocabulary words. Let them know that in this story *giant* means "really big." Lead them to express another meaning for *giant* (*A large imaginary person*).

TARGET SKILL AND STRATEGY

PLOT AND THEME Discuss that every story has a "big idea." Tell children that as they read *A Big Change*, they should think about what the author is saying about moving from one place to another. Then remind children that the plot is what happens in the story. Have children tell what is happening in each of the illustrations and how Jen might be feeling. Guide them to see how the events in each picture can be related to the pictures that come before it and after it.

SUMMARIZE Work with children to create a story chart that shows the beginning, middle, and end. Let them know they will be filling it in after reading. Tell them that since they will only be writing a couple of sentences in each section of the chart, they will need to decide which are the most important ideas in each part.

ADDITIONAL SKILL INSTRUCTION

REALISM AND FANTASY Remind children that a realistic story tells about something that could happen and a fantasy is a story about something that could not happen. As children read *A Big Change* have them decide if the things in the story could all really happen. After reading, have children tell you if the story was a realistic one or a fantasy and why.

Name _____

Plot and Theme

Every story has a beginning, middle, and end. Draw pictures in the boxes to show the beginning, middle, and end of *A Big Change*. Write a sentence or two under each box to tell what is happening.

1. | **Beginning** |

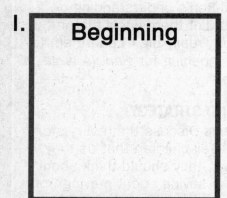

2. | **Middle** |

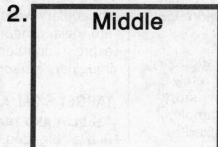

3. | **End** |

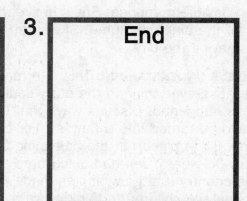

Think about what happened in *A Big Change* and how Jen felt. What do you think is the "Big Idea" of this story? Write your answer below.

4. _____

_____

_____

_____

_____

Name _____

Vocabulary

Choose words from the word box to complete the sentences.

Words to Know			
block	chuckle	fair	giant
strong	tears	trouble	

1. I could not eat all of the _____ slice of pie.

2. There are lots of houses on my _____.

3. You have to be _____ to lift that heavy box.

4. It's not _____ that I have to clean up while my sister watches TV!

Write a sentence for each of the following words:

chuckle   tears   trouble

5. _____

6. _____

7. _____

Special Beach Day

SUMMARY In this fictional account, children learn how a family's day at the beach is affected by a sudden thunderstorm. Children learn some simple facts and dangers of thunderstorms, but also discover that such storms often pass quickly.

LESSON VOCABULARY

angry	branches
clung	finger
picnic	pressing
special	

INTRODUCE THE BOOK

INTRODUCE THE TITLE AND AUTHOR Discuss with children the title and the author of *Special Beach Day*. Have children look at the cover illustration. Ask: Who do you think these people are? What are they doing?

BUILD BACKGROUND Discuss what children know about thunderstorms. Ask if any of them have ever been caught outdoors in a thunderstorm and if so, how they and their families coped.

PREVIEW Ask children to look through the book and predict what the story will be about, using the pictures as guides. Direct children to page 12 and discuss why a photograph has been used here instead of drawings. Explain that this page is giving factual information and is not part of the story about the family at the beach.

READ THE BOOK

SET PURPOSE Have children set a purpose for reading *Special Beach Day*. If children need help with this, ask: What do you want to learn from this story? Do you want to learn about the family? Do you want to learn why their day at the beach is special?

STRATEGY SUPPORT: ASK QUESTIONS Encourage children to ask questions as they read *Special Beach Day*. Model how to ask questions. For example, have children turn to page 3 and ask: I wonder what's in the basket next to the woman?

COMPREHENSION QUESTIONS

PAGE 3 What is the weather like in the picture on this page? *(It's sunny.)*

PAGE 7 What has happened to the weather now? *(A storm is moving in.)*

PAGES 5, 7 Why is the family going towards the tree on page 5? Why have they moved away from the tree on page 7? *(On page 5, they are going toward the tree to get in the shade. On page 7, they have moved away from the tree in order to take shelter in the car.)*

PAGES 8-9 Why doesn't the mother drive the children home? *(Possible response: The mother probably has had experience with storms and predicts that the storm will pass quickly so she and her family can return to the beach.)*

PAGE 12 What are some facts that you learned about thunderstorms on this page? *(Possible responses: Thunderstorms can produce lightning; thunderstorms are difficult to predict; to stay safe, find shelter indoors and stay away from windows.)*

REVISIT THE BOOK

READER RESPONSE

1. Fact: It's safer in the car; it's not smart to be under tree branches when there is lightning. Opinion: "The storm is cool."
2. Possible responses: What makes lightning happen? Why isn't it safe to use a telephone during a thunderstorm?
3. Responses will vary but should reflect understanding of the meaning of vocabulary words as used in the story.
4. Possible response: Tony or Lisa could have been harmed by high waves.

EXTEND UNDERSTANDING Have a volunteer demonstrate to the class what he or she thinks it means to "sound angry." Then remind children that on page 7, Tony said that the "sky sounds angry." Have them discuss what they think this means.

RESPONSE OPTIONS

WRITING Ask children to write about the last thunderstorm they remember. Encourage them to use the 5 Ws—*what, when, who, where, why*—and *how* to help them describe this experience.

SCIENCE CONNECTION

Tell children that when lightning strikes nearby, they can almost immediately hear the thunder. However, when lightning strikes far away, they will see the flash of light but it will be a few seconds before they hear the thunder. Have children try to explain why this might be so. (*Light travels faster than sound.*)

Skill Work

TEACH/REVIEW VOCABULARY

On the chalkboard, list the vocabulary words except for *pressing* and *clung*. Discuss which words name things and which describe things.

ELL Ask children to share weather words from other languages (for example, the words for *lightning, storm, hurricane, tornado* and *thunder*). Discuss words that sound similar to English words of the same meaning. (Spanish for *hurricane* is *huracán*). Also discuss words that sound very different from their English counterparts. (In Spanish, *lightning* is *rayo* or *relámpago*).

TARGET SKILL AND STRATEGY

FACT AND OPINION Remind children that a statement of *fact* can be proven true or false. (*Example: My birthday is on July 22.*) A statement of opinion expresses a person's feelings or beliefs. (*Example: Everyone loves birthdays.*) Have each child create and say one statement of fact and one statement of opinion.

ASK QUESTIONS Explain to children that we ask questions to get information. Sometimes one of the questions we ask about the information we get is: "Is this a fact or is this an opinion?" We use all this information to make decisions. Have children identify some questions they would like to have answered about thunderstorms.

ADDITIONAL SKILL INSTRUCTION

CAUSE AND EFFECT As children read, remind them to think about things that happen and why those things happen. Explain that sometimes clue words like *so* and *because* can help them name the *cause* and *effect*. For example, in "Raj was hungry so he ate a sandwich," what happened is that Raj ate a sandwich (*effect*), and the reason he did this was because he was hungry (*cause*). Ask children to find at least one effect and its cause in Special Beach Day.

Name _____

Fact and Opinion

Decide whether each sentence below is a statement of fact or of opinion. Underline your choice.

1. Sunscreen protects your skin on sunny days.

    FACT   OPINION

2. Walking on sand is hard.

    FACT   OPINION

3. It is not smart to be under a tree where there is lightning.

    FACT   OPINION

4. Lightning can strike tree branches.

    FACT   OPINION

5. "I think the storm is cool!"

    FACT   OPINION

6. "The sky sounds angry."

    FACT   OPINION

7. "It stopped raining."

    FACT   OPINION

8. Thunderstorms can have lightning and thunder.

    FACT   OPINION

9. There is nothing better than a beach day!

    FACT   OPINION

10. Ocean waves are sometimes high after a storm.

    FACT   OPINION

Name _____

Vocabulary

Use a word from the box to complete each sentence.

Words to Know			
angry	branches	clung	finger
picnic	pressing	special	

1. The wind blew and the tree _____ shook.

2. It can be fun to enjoy a _____ on a nice summer day.

3. A clap of thunder made the boy say, "The sky sounds _____."

4. During the storm, the girl _____ to her cat to feel safe.

5. The little boy pointed his _____ at the big sign.

6. The children were _____ their noses against the glass to see if the rain had stopped.

7. Even with the storm, the children had a very _____ day at the beach.

Community Helpers

SUMMARY Many people live and work in a community. From police officers to firefighters, from teachers to doctors and mail carriers, the people who work in a community help each other, as well as other people who live in the community.

LESSON VOCABULARY

buildings	burning
masks	quickly
roar	station
tightly	

INTRODUCE THE BOOK

INTRODUCE THE TITLE AND AUTHOR Before reading the title, ask children to identify the professions they see on the book cover. Confirm for children that they see a police officer, a doctor, and a mail carrier. Then, ask children what all these people have in common and lead children to the idea that all these people work in a community. Turn children's attention to the book title and author. Let children predict other community helpers they might meet in the book.

BUILD BACKGROUND Say the word *community* and invite children to say the first words that pop into their minds. Record children's ideas on chart paper. Encourage children to explain and describe what the word *community* means to them. Help children conclude that communities are places where people live and work. Many people work in a community to help make the community a good place to live.

PREVIEW/TAKE A PICTURE WALK Encourage children to look through the book and identify the community workers they see. In addition, have children identify the tools that each community worker uses. For example, on page 5, which police officer's tool do children see? *(a police car)* What firefighter's tool do they see on pages 6-7? *(the firefighter's protective suit, helmet, and fire truck)*

READ THE BOOK

SET PURPOSE Work with children to set a purpose for reading. Ask children what they would like to learn from reading this book and write their ideas on the board. Encourage children to pose any questions too. Direct children to look for the answers to their questions as they read. For example, perhaps children would like to learn which community workers help children.

STRATEGY SUPPORT: TEXT STRUCTURE Mention to children that as they read, it often helps to think about the way the book is organized, or the text structure. Explain that in this book, you would like them to think about the order in which things happen. For example, what happens when a firefighter gets a call about a fire? What happens after first-aid workers respond to an emergency? What sequence does a mail carrier follow?

COMPREHENSION QUESTIONS

PAGE 4 What is the main idea of this page? *(Communities need people to help the community.)*

PAGE 8 What might be the sequence of events for this teacher during one day? *(The teacher gets up, goes to school, prepares for class, teaches the students, grades papers, goes home, eats dinner.)*

PAGE 10 Why do communities need first-aid workers? *(To help people who are hurt or sick)*

PAGE 12 Why does the author think you might know librarians? *(Some librarians work in schools and help children find books.)*

REVISIT THE BOOK

READER RESPONSE

1. Possible response: Community workers help people who live in a community.
2. Possible responses: First, the firefighters get their masks and hoses. Then, they jump into their fire truck. They drive to the fire. They rescue people and put out the fire.
3. Possible responses: police station, fire station, library, school, hospital, post office
4. Possible responses: helmet, protective jacket and pants, truck with crane and ladder.

EXTEND UNDERSTANDING Ask children to think about the ways that community workers are all connected. For example, a mail carrier delivers the mail to other community workers. First-aid workers might help coaches if a player gets hurt. Coaches might coach kids whose parents are firefighters. Librarians might help doctors find books about medicine. After making connections, prompt children to conclude that community workers all help each other.

RESPONSE OPTIONS

WRITING Ask students to choose one job in this book that interests them. Have children write a few sentences that explains why they might someday like to do this job.

SPEAKING Suggest to children that a community worker visits their class. What might the community worker say? What might the community worker talk about? Working in groups, have children role-play being community workers, talking about their jobs. Monitor the groups to make sure children stay on task and include details from the book.

SOCIAL STUDIES CONNECTION

Time For SOCIAL STUDIES

Divide the class into groups, one for each worker in this book. Have children research the training each job requires. Guide their research in books or over the Internet. Invite groups to report their findings back to the class.

Skill Work

TEACH/REVIEW VOCABULARY

Write the vocabulary words on the board, and read them with the class. Provide a contextual sentence for each word. Have children explain the meaning of each word based on the way they used it in the sentence.

ELL Show children a picture of a burning building. Label parts of the picture to introduce the vocabulary words, such as *building, burning,* and *masks* worn by firefighters. Act out other words, such as *quickly, roar,* and *tightly.* For the word *station,* show children a picture of a police station or fire station.

TARGET SKILL AND STRATEGY

MAIN IDEA Review with children that the *main idea* of something is what that section is mostly about. Read page 3 with the group and ask children to identify the main idea of this page. *(What is a community?)*

TEXT STRUCTURE Share with children that *text structure* is the way information is organized. In this reader, information is organized according to the different roles community workers play. Have children cite examples to show why this is so.

ADDITIONAL SKILL INSTRUCTION

COMPARE/CONTRAST Remind children that when you *compare* two or more things, you show how they are alike. When you *contrast* two or more things, you show how they are different. Invite children to choose two community workers in the book to compare and contrast.

Name _____

Main Idea

Read the paragraph below.

> Police officers patrol their communities using cars, bicycles, or horses. They make sure everyone is safe. Some police officers direct traffic. Police officers help the people in a community live together in peace.

What is the main idea of this paragraph? Write your ideas below.

_____

_____

_____

_____

_____

_____

_____

_____

_____

_____

Name _____

Vocabulary

Choose a word from the box that best fits in each sentence.

Words to Know
buildings   burning   masks   quickly roar   station   tightly

1. The alarm went off at the fire _____ .

2. The firemen dressed _____ and rushed to the fire engine.

3. The fire spread to three apartment _____ .

4. The firemen wore _____ on their faces to help them breathe.

5. They gripped the hose _____ .

6. People could hear the fire _____ .

7. The firemen rushed into the _____ building.

Horse Rescue!

SUMMARY The U.S. Coast Guard is mostly known for rescuing people and animals when they are in danger on the sea. On March 7, 2001, the Coast Guard was called in to rescue 16 horses that had become trapped by floodwaters in Louisiana. This book takes readers through that daring rescue, which included not only boats, but helicopters as well.

LESSON VOCABULARY

flashes	lightning	pounded
poured	rolling	storm
thunder		

INTRODUCE THE BOOK

INTRODUCE THE TITLE AND AUTHOR Have children identify the animal on the cover, then ask children if they see the word *horse* in the book title. Confirm that the word does appear, then read the book title and author name with them. Discuss the meaning of the word *rescue,* and elicit ideas for what a *horse* rescue might be. Encourage children to consider how a horse might get in trouble or why a horse might need to be rescued.

BUILD BACKGROUND Invite children to share their knowledge of horses. Ask children if they consider horses to be land animals or water animals. (Children should describe horses as land animals.) Ask children what might happen if horses became stuck in rising waters from a flood. Let students predict outcomes to check after reading.

PREVIEW/TAKE A PICTURE WALK Invite children to look through the book and point out images that surprised them. For example, children might be surprised to see the horse and the helicopter on pages 10 and 11. Have children explain why this image is surprising, and ask children why the helicopter might be carrying the horse.

READ THE BOOK

SET PURPOSE After discussing the cover and book title, ask children why they would want to read this book. Elicit ideas. For example, children want to learn how the horses got in trouble or how they are rescued. Tell children that discovering the answers to these questions is setting a purpose for reading. Encourage children to look for the answers as they read.

STRATEGY SUPPORT: GRAPHIC ORGANIZERS Suggest that children draw a time line to help them recognize the sequence of events in this book. At the beginning of the time line, tell them to write "The horses are trapped in the water." After they read each page, ask children to pause and to write on their time lines what happens next. After reading, review children's time lines, and ask children if they found completing the time line helpful for understanding the book.

COMPREHENSION QUESTIONS

PAGE 5 What sequence is being described on this page? *(How the land flooded and the horses became trapped)*

PAGE 5 Use a time line to show the sequence of events on this page. *(It rained for a long time. The rivers filled up. Then, water came onto the land. The land began to flood. The farmers tried to rescue the horses. The horses became trapped.)*

PAGE 6 Why did the farmers call the Coast Guard? *(To rescue the horses; because they knew the Coast Guard were experts at water rescue)*

PAGE 10 What is a sling? *(a loop of material you can use to pick something up; the picture shows a sling)*

REVISIT THE BOOK

READER RESPONSE

1. It rained for so long that the rivers overflowed and flooded the land.
2. They flew over the horses. A person went into the water to place a sling around each horse. The helicopters lifted the horses to dry land.
3. Possible response: bursts of lightning
4. Possible response: The illustration shows what the sling is like.

EXTEND UNDERSTANDING Talk with students about the emotions of the people—and even the animals—in the book. Ask children to think about how the owner of the horses might feel; how the rescue workers feel; how the horses feel. You might call attention to illustrations to prompt ideas. Discuss how exploring the feelings of the people and animals in the book gives readers a clearer understanding of what is happening.

RESPONSE OPTIONS

WRITING Tell children to imagine they are interviewing the Coast Guard members who saved the horses. What questions might they ask? How might the Coast Guard answer? Ask children to write questions and answers, using information from the book.

SCIENCE CONNECTION

TIME FOR Science

Remind children that most horses are domesticated animals, meaning people raise and care for them. Ask children what kind of shelter they think would be best for horses, and have children explain their ideas.

Skill Work

TEACH/REVIEW VOCABULARY

Write the words on the board for children to read and invite children to use the words in sentences to tell about storms they've experienced or imagined.

ELL Ask children to draw a picture of a rain storm, with dark clouds and lightning. Help children label their pictures with vocabulary words. Demonstrate *pours, pounds,* and *flashes* through hand motions; for example, *pound* on a table, *pour* water from one cup to another, and *flash* your fingers open to indicate a burst of light.

TARGET SKILL AND STRATEGY

SEQUENCE Explain that *sequence* is the order in which things happen. Have children read page 3. Talk about the sequence of events that would prompt the Coast Guard to rescue someone (*storm comes up suddenly; people or animals are in danger; someone calls Coast Guard; Coast Guard arrives; Coast Guard rescues people*).

GRAPHIC ORGANIZERS Review for children that *graphic organizers* are tools to present information in new ways. Share some graphic organizers that children already use (word webs, Venn diagrams, and flow charts). Explain that a time line is a graphic organizer that shows a sequence. Work with children to complete a time line for the sequence they described on page 3.

ADDITIONAL SKILL INSTRUCTION

FACT AND OPINION Mention to children that a *fact* can be proved either true or false. An *opinion,* however, expresses what someone thinks or feels; opinions cannot be proven true or false. Read the following sentence, and have children distinguish fact from opinion. Page 4: "The farm was normally a sunny place with pretty hills." Fact: The farm has hills. Opinion: The hills are pretty. Invite children to look for facts and opinions from the book.

Name _____

Sequence

Number the sentences below from 1 to 7 to show the sequence of the horse rescue.

Hint: Look for clue words, like **first** and **finally**.

_____

_____ Next, the Coast Guard lowered a person down to each big horse.

_____ Helicopters flew to the place where the horses were last seen.

_____ Finally, an animal doctor checked the horses.

_____ The Coast Guard loaded the smaller horses onto a boat.

_____ Then the person put a sling around the big horse.

_____ First, the farmers called the U.S. Coast Guard for help.

_____ The helicopters flew the big horses to safety.

© Pearson Education 2

Name _____

Vocabulary

Find these words in the puzzle. They can be across, up, or down.

flashes	lightning	pounded	poured
rolling	storm	thunder	

```
L  I  G  H  T  N  I  N  G
F  L  A  S  H  E  S  L  N
O  O  P  O  U  R  E  D  I
K  P  O  U  N  D  E  D  L
A  T  T  H  D  E  S  K  L
Y  H  O  R  E  S  E  S  O
F  S  T  O  R  M  L  Y  R
```

Now write the leftover letters in order on the lines below to reveal a secret message.

__ __ __ __ __ __ __ __ __

__ __ __ !

__ __ __ __ __ __ __ __ __ __ !

Sally and the Wild Puppy

SUMMARY This story is about Sally and her new puppy, Sparks. At first Sparks is very wild, but, after some training and practice, he begins to learn how to behave.

LESSON VOCABULARY

chased	chewing
dripping	grabbed
practice	treat
wagged	

INTRODUCE THE BOOK

INTRODUCE THE TITLE AND AUTHOR Discuss with children the title and the author of *Sally and the Wild Puppy*. Ask children what they think the author might mean by "wild." Have them describe what they see happening in the cover illustration. Ask: How does this illustration relate to the title? What is wild about this puppy? What do you think the puppy's owner will think of his behavior?

BUILD BACKGROUND Engage children in a discussion of puppies and invite them to share what they know. Ask: Why do you think so many people like puppies? What are the different things that puppies do? Why do puppies get in trouble? What can owners do to keep puppies from being wild like the one on the cover of this book?

PREVIEW Have children preview the book, looking at the illustrations. Invite them to describe what is happening on each page and predict what the text will be about. Ask: What is the puppy doing here? Is he being good or bad? How does the girl, Sally, feel about her puppy? What tells you this? How can Sally help her puppy behave?

READ THE BOOK

SET PURPOSE Model for children how to set a purpose for reading. Use the cover illustration to pique children's interest. Say: "On the cover, I see that this very wild puppy has made a big mess and knocked over a lamp and a chair. I'd like to know why he did this and why he is called the "wild" puppy. I'm going to read to find out."

STRATEGY SUPPORT: PRIOR KNOWLEDGE As children read, prompt them to use their prior knowledge to understand what is happening in the story. After reading page 7, ask: What does Sparks do each time Sally gives him a command? Why does Sparks do this? What do you know about puppies that tells you this? Continue in the same manner throughout the book.

COMPREHENSION QUESTIONS

PAGE 3 What does Grandma Betty mean by "a special treat"? *(a surprise or present)*

PAGE 5 What are some of the things that Sparks has already done? How do you think Sally and Grandma feel about it? *(Sparks has made a mess, bumped the chairs, and knocked over plants. Sally and Grandma might be angry or irritated.)*

PAGE 8 Why do you think Sally gives Sparks hugs when he obeys? *(because Sally is happy with Sparks, wants to encourage him, wants him to continue to obey)*

PAGE 9 Why didn't Sally mind that Sparks still chewed on her slippers? *(because he had stopped chewing on chairs)*

PAGE 11 Why was Sparks so good by the end of the story? *(because Sally had practiced with him and he learned how to behave and obey)*

REVISIT THE BOOK

READER RESPONSE

1. Theme: Training a puppy. Beginning: Sally gets a new puppy; Middle: Sparks is disobedient; End: Sally trains Sparks.
2. Responses will vary, but children should be encouraged to activate their prior knowledge about practicing.
3. A *treat* is a small gift or reward. Sally might give her puppy a bone.
4. Responses should reflect comprehension of plot.

EXTEND UNDERSTANDING Explain to children that a character is a person or an animal in a story. Have them describe what they know about Sally based on the illustrations and text. Encourage them to describe both physical characteristics as well as personality traits. Ask: What does Sally look like? How old do you think she is? Does Sally like Sparks, even though he is wild? Sally practices a lot with Sparks. What does this tell you about her?

RESPONSE OPTIONS

SPEAKING Help children retell the story by recalling the main events from the beginning, middle, and end of the book. Use a graphic organizer, and write down these main events for children to use as a reference. Working in pairs, children can practice retelling the story to each other. Encourage children to be expressive, using as many details and descriptive words as possible.

ART CONNECTION

Have children illustrate two events from the story by choosing one good thing and one bad thing that Sparks did. Children can label their illustrations with *good* and *bad* and post their drawings to share with the rest of the class.

Skill Work

TEACH/REVIEW VOCABULARY

Play a game of charades by having children take turns acting out and guessing the vocabulary words. As children guess each word correctly, help them write it down on their own paper. To aid comprehension, offer a few different sentences using each word, for example: *After swimming, I was* dripping *wet. The leaky faucet was* dripping.

TARGET SKILL AND STRATEGY

THEME AND PLOT Explain to children that every story has a "big idea" or a *theme*. Before reading, invite children to predict what the story is all about, or what we might learn about. Remind them to think about what the big idea might be as they read. Tell children that keeping track of the main events of the story will help them determine the theme. After reading, use the first Reader Response question to review and discuss the theme and main events in the book.

PRIOR KNOWLEDGE Before reading, use your discussion of puppies to encourage children to activate their existing knowledge of the subject. Ask: What do you know about puppies that might help you better understand this story? How did you use your knowledge of puppies to understand what the author meant by the "wild" puppy?

ELL Have children describe or act out the meaning of *wild* for greater comprehension. As they do so, encourage children to say the word in their native languages as well as in English.

ADDITIONAL SKILL INSTRUCTION

CAUSE AND EFFECT As you read pages 4 and 5, have children explain what has happened and why. Ask: What has happened here? Why do you think Sparks created such a mess? What does the text say? What does the illustration show? Do you think Sparks did this on purpose?

Name _____

Theme and Plot

Sally and the Wild Puppy is all about training a puppy. Circle the three events from the story that best relate to training a puppy. Then write "beginning," "middle," or "end" next to the circled events to tell when they happened in the story.

_____

_____   1. Sparks learned to obey and became a good listener.

_____

_____   2. Grandma gave Sally a puppy.

_____

_____   3. Sparks made a big mess.

_____

_____   4. Sally practiced with Sparks.

_____

_____   5. Sally was happy to get a puppy.

In the space below, draw a picture that shows the theme of *Sally and the Wild Puppy.*

Name _____

Vocabulary

Choose a word from the box that best fits in each sentence.

Words to Know

chased	chewing	dripping	grabbed
practice	treat	wagged	

1. Grandma said she had a special _____ for Sally.

2. Sally's puppy was _____ everything in sight.

3. The puppy's tail _____ so hard that it was blurry.

4. Sally wanted Sparks to _____ to become the perfect puppy.

5. Sparks _____ after Sally.

6. Sally _____ Sparks as he ran out the door.

7. Sparks liked to give sloppy, _____ licks.

What an Adventure!

SUMMARY This nonfiction book describes how children can express friendship through an adventure club. It supports and extends the lesson concept of being a good friend and neighbor.

LESSON VOCABULARY

adventure   climbed
clubhouses   exploring
greatest   truest
wondered

INTRODUCE THE BOOK

INTRODUCE THE TITLE AND AUTHOR Discuss with children the title and author of *What an Adventure!* Explain that social studies includes learning about how people act with each other. Ask: How might this book relate to social studies?

BUILD BACKGROUND Have children give examples of an adventure. Ask: Have you ever had an adventure with a friend? Invite children to share their experiences.

PREVIEW/TAKE A PICTURE WALK Have children look at the photos, captions, and labels in the book before reading. Ask children to discuss how those text features relate to the title of the book.

READ THE BOOK

SET PURPOSE Have children set a purpose for reading *What an Adventure!* Remind children of what they discussed in the preview. You may need to work with children to have them set their own purpose. Ask: Would you like to know what happens in an adventure club? Do you want to know what adventures you can have with your friends?

STRATEGY SUPPORT: ASK QUESTIONS Remind children that good readers ask questions about what they are reading to predict, understand, find information, discover new information, and think about what they have learned. Model questions or reflections. Before: I wonder what this will be about? I really want to know about . . . . I hope the author will talk about . . . . During: I wonder what this means. I'll read it again to find out. What does this word mean? I'll finish the sentence to find out. I like this. How did the author make it so exciting? After: What did I like best? The author didn't cover everything. I wonder where I can learn more about . . . . Explain to children that the signal words *who, what, when, where, why,* and *how* are good question starters. Encourage children to use a KWL chart to generate questions about this book. Help children learn to use the chart by filling in the "K" section as a class.

COMPREHENSION QUESTIONS

PAGE 4 Why else would you join an adventure club? *(Possible response: to learn new things or to have fun)*

PAGE 6 Why does canoeing take teamwork? *(Everyone in the canoe needs to row together.)*

PAGES 6–7 Why are visiting a mountain, canoeing, and sailing included in a book about adventures? *(Possible response: They are unusual and exciting.)*

PAGE 10 Why does the author tell you about city clubs? *(Possible response: It might be hard for some kids to have trips outside the city.)*

REVISIT THE BOOK

THINK AND SHARE

1. She wants you to join an adventure club.
2. Possible response: K: You do it in a river. W: What is white water rafting like? L: White water rafting is exciting.
3. *club* and *house*; knowing this helps us remember that a clubhouse is a place where club members feel at home.
4. Possible response: Teamwork is important in group adventure activities.

EXTEND UNDERSTANDING Point out the captions. Ask: How do the captions help you understand the photos? Guide children to see how they help connect the photos to the text.

RESPONSE OPTIONS

VIEWING Have children look at the photos and describe what skills might be needed for each activity.

SOCIAL STUDIES CONNECTION

Time For SOCIAL STUDIES

Have small groups of children work together to draw up a plan for an adventure club. Have them consider the club's purpose, where and when it will meet, how it will be funded, and how they can get adults to help.

Skill Work

TEACH/REVIEW VOCABULARY

Give children vocabulary word cards. Have them sort the words into groups of three-, two-, and one-syllable words.

ELL Have children place the vocabulary word cards face down in a pile. They take turns picking up a card and making up a riddle for the others to guess. Have them use these patterns: This word starts with the letter _____. This word ends with the letter _____.

TARGET SKILL AND STRATEGY

AUTHOR'S PURPOSE During the preview, ask: Who wrote this book? What do you think the book will be about? What do you think the book will be like—funny, sad, interesting, exciting? Why? After reading, ask: Were you right about what the book is about? Were you right about the book being exciting? Finally, ask questions related to the author's purpose: On page 8, why does the author include a picture of children in a raft? Why does the author talk directly to you, the reader?

ASK QUESTIONS Remind children that good readers ask questions as they read to predict, understand, think about what they have learned, and discover the author's purpose. Model questioning. Before: I wonder what this will be about? During: I wonder what this means. I'll read it again to find out. After: I wonder where I can learn more about…

ADDITIONAL SKILL INSTRUCTION

DRAW CONCLUSIONS Tell children that as they read, they can use what they have read and seen and what they already know to figure out more about what happens in the book. Model: "On page 4, I see that outdoor gear includes a sleeping bag. Based on what I read and what I know, I think that adventure clubs might include overnight trips." After page 6, ask: Why does everyone in a canoe need to row together?

Name_____

Author's Purpose

Think about why the author wrote *What an Adventure!* Read each question below. Then underline the best answer.

1. Why does the author say that you can join an adventure club?
  a. to get you to do something
  b. to show how to do something
  c. to make you feel good

2. Why does the author show you camping tools?
  a. to get you to buy them
  b. to tell you about camping
  c. to teach you about the tools

3. Why does the author say that sailing is a lot of fun?
  a. to prove that sailing is better than camping
  b. to teach us about sailing
  c. to get us excited about sailing

4. Why does the author describe what adventure clubs do?
  a. to prove they are the best clubs
  b. to teach us about them
  c. to make us feel bad

5. Why did the author write this book?
  a. to get us to try an adventure club
  b. to make us laugh
  c. to help us take a test

© Pearson Education 2

Name_____

Vocabulary

Draw a line to match each word with its clue.

1. adventure   a. places to meet

2. climbed   b. most loyal

3. clubhouses   c. went up

4. exploring   d. an exciting time

5. greatest   e. had a question

6. truest   f. the most

7. wondered   g. looking for new things

Grandpa's Sign

SUMMARY Andrew breaks a sign his grandfather made, and then tries to hide the pieces so no one will know. When his father finds the broken pieces, Andrew confesses and promises to be more careful, and more honest, next time.

LESSON VOCABULARY

afternoon	blame
ideas	important
signmaker	townspeople

INTRODUCE THE BOOK

INTRODUCE THE TITLE AND AUTHOR Discuss with children the title and the author of *Grandpa's Sign*. Based on the title, ask children to say what they think the book will be about.

BUILD BACKGROUND Invite children to talk about their own experiences with doing something that they know is wrong. Ask them to tell how they felt when they did something they knew was wrong. Ask them to say what happened afterwards, and have them explain what they learned from their mistakes.

PREVIEW/TAKE A PICTURE WALK As children preview the book, have them notice the illustrations and the feature with the photo on page 12. Ask them to make predictions about what the story will be about, based on these text features.

ELL Page through the story and point to details in the illustrations. Invite children to identify objects on pages 3–5. Invite them to explain what happens on pages 6–9. Invite them to read the signs in the picture on pages 10–11. Bring in some examples of other common signs, and have children tell, in their native language, the words for those signs.

READ THE BOOK

SET PURPOSE Have children set a purpose for reading *Grandpa's Sign*. Children's interest in knowing the consequences of doing the wrong thing should guide this purpose.

STRATEGY SUPPORT: MONITOR AND FIX UP Tell children that as they read they may come to parts that don't make sense. Remind them that this is not unusual. Encourage them to reread those portions of the text that they find confusing.

COMPREHENSION QUESTIONS

PAGE 3 Why was today an important day for Andrew and his family? *(They were having a yard sale.)*

PAGE 4 Why was Andrew excited? *(He wanted to earn money by selling some of his old toys.)*

PAGE 5 What did Andrew's grandfather use to paint his signs on? *(glass)*

PAGE 6 Could what happens on this page really happen in real life? *(yes)*

PAGE 7 How did Andrew feel about hiding the broken sign? *(bad)*

PAGE 9 Why do you think Andrew didn't tell anyone about breaking Grandpa's sign? *(Possible response: He didn't want to get blamed or punished.)*

REVISIT THE BOOK

READER RESPONSE

1. Possible response: Yes, I think the story could really happen, because people do have yard sales.
2. Answers should include Andrew looking at sign; noticing a customer; dropping sign on table; sign sliding off table and smashing.
3. No one would know who was responsible.
4. Answers will vary but encourage children to empathize with Andrew's plight while acknowledging that being careful and honest is important.

EXTEND UNDERSTANDING Have children describe their favorite illustrations in the book. Have them compare the illustration on pages 8 and 9 to the photo on page 12. Ask: How are they similar? Ask: What do you think Andrew is thinking in the illustration? What do you think the girl is thinking in the photo?

RESPONSE OPTIONS

SPEAKING Invite children to say what they think the big idea of this story is. Challenge them to put their idea into one sentence. Remind them that each reader may interpret the big idea of the story differently, based on his or her own experiences. Challenge children to back up their statement of the big idea with details from the story.

ART CONNECTION

Children may wish to write their own realistic stories about a time when they did something they knew was wrong. Challenge them to "make a book" and to illustrate the pages. Have them tell what happened and how they felt about it. You may wish to make an exhibit of the books.

Skill Work

TEACH/REVIEW VOCABULARY

Have children look up the meaning of the word blame. Invite them to use the word in a sentence. Continue in a similar fashion with the remaining vocabulary words.

TARGET SKILL AND STRATEGY

REALISM AND FANTASY Remind children that a *realistic* story tells about something that could happen. A *fantasy* is a story about something that could not happen. Invite children to look for details as they read that help them decide whether it is a realistic story or a fantasy.

MONITOR AND FIX UP Remind children that a good reader knows reading has to make sense. If reading stops making sense, a good reader has some fix-up strategies to help him or her get back to understanding. Tell children to think about these questions as they read: Who is the story about? Where does the story happen? When does it happen? What happens in the beginning, middle, and end of the story? Explain that these questions can also help them determine whether the story is a realistic one or a fantasy.

ADDITIONAL SKILL INSTRUCTION

THEME After children read the book, ask: What is the big idea of this story? When you read this story, what did you learn about people? How does this story remind you of something that happened in your family or school? Encourage children to think about how the story relates to them as readers.

Name _____

Realism and Fantasy

Read each question below. Then circle your answer.

1. Are there things in the story that could not really happen?

   yes   no

2. Is there magic in the story?

   yes   no

3. Could things in the story really happen?

   yes   no

4. Do the people in the story do and say things like people I know?

   yes   no

5. Write one sentence that tells if the story *Grandpa's Sign* is a realistic story or fantasy. Tell how you know.

   _____

   -

   _____

   _____

   -

   _____

   _____

   -

   _____

Name _____

Vocabulary

Draw a line to match the word parts and make words from the story.

l. idea   a. maker

2. impor   b. tant

3. sign   c. noon

4. towns   d. people

5. after   e. s

6. Write a sentence with the word *blame*.

_____

_____

_____

_____

Three of the Greats

SUMMARY This nonfiction text explores the lives and careers of three great African American baseball players: Satchel Paige, James Bell, and Josh Gibson.

LESSON VOCABULARY

bases	cheers
field	plate
sailed	threw

INTRODUCE THE BOOK

INTRODUCE THE TITLE AND AUTHOR Discuss with children the title and author of *Three of the Greats*. Ask: Do you know who any of these people are on the cover? What do you think they do or did? What tells you that? Discuss the "Biography" label in the upper-right corner and what it means. Say: A biography is a book of information about a real person or people. Who or what do you think this book will be about? What do you think the author means by *Three of the Greats*?

BUILD BACKGROUND Engage children in a discussion of baseball. Have them share what they know about the sport as well as their experiences playing or watching the game. Ask: What things do you usually see at a baseball game? What happens during a baseball game? Who are some of your favorite baseball players?

PREVIEW/TAKE A PICTURE WALK Have children preview the book, looking at the photographs. Call special attention to the photographs on pages 6, 7, and 11. Point out the labels on the photographs, and help children say the names of these players. Ask: What do you think these three men have to do with this book? How do you think they relate to the title of the book?

READ THE BOOK

SET PURPOSE Model for the children how to set a purpose for reading. Say: The title of this book is *Three of the Greats*, and there are three men pictured on the cover. I'm guessing that they are the "three greats" the author is referring to. But why are they called great? What did they do? That's what I want to find out by reading this book.

STRATEGY SUPPORT: VISUALIZE As they read, encourage children to continue forming pictures in their minds in order to better understand the text. Pause after reading page 10. Have children describe the images they think of when they read about people saying that Josh Gibson must have hit the ball over 200 miles.

COMPREHENSION QUESTIONS

PAGE 3 How was baseball in the past different from today? (*African American players were not allowed to play in the major leagues. They played in separate baseball leagues called the Negro leagues.*)

PAGE 4 Why were African American baseball players not allowed to join the major leagues? (*because of their skin color*)

PAGE 6 What team did Satchel Paige help win the World Series? What year? (*Cleveland Indians, 1948*)

PAGE 11 How many home runs did Josh Gibson hit? (*almost 800*)

PAGE 12 How have Satchel Paige, James Bell, and Josh Gibson been honored for their skill? (*They have been included in the Baseball Hall of Fame.*)

REVISIT THE BOOK

READER RESPONSE

1. Responses may vary but should include the fact that today, African American baseball players play on major league teams and in the past they played in the Negro leagues. Use the chart to organize your ideas.
2. Responses may vary but should reflect an understanding of James Bell's speed.
3. Responses may vary but should reflect comprehension of word meanings in the context of baseball.
4. Responses may vary, but should include that these were skilled players who made the game of baseball very exciting.

EXTEND UNDERSTANDING Call children's attention to the section headings that introduce each baseball player. Discuss with children how these headings help organize the book and tell us what information is going to come next. Ask: If you wanted to find specific information about James Bell, where would you look? Which page and heading mark the beginning of the section on Satchel Paige?

RESPONSE OPTIONS

WRITING Provide children with more information about other important and famous baseball players, of any race, past and present. Have each child choose one baseball player to study, and then gather information from books as well as the Internet. Have children write short lists of information about their players that include statistics and accomplishments such as position, team, World Series games, Hall of Fame, etc. Children may also draw pictures of their players to display along with their written lists.

SOCIAL STUDIES CONNECTION

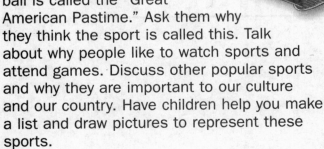

Tell children that baseball is called the "Great American Pastime." Ask them why they think the sport is called this. Talk about why people like to watch sports and attend games. Discuss other popular sports and why they are important to our culture and our country. Have children help you make a list and draw pictures to represent these sports.

Skill Work

TEACH/REVIEW VOCABULARY

Say each of the vocabulary words aloud with the children and discuss the definitions. Ask children what they think these words have in common. Remind children of your discussion about baseball, and use these words in context as you describe the sights and sounds of a baseball game.

ELL Use photographs or pantomime to help English language learners understand the meanings of the vocabulary words.

TARGET SKILL AND STRATEGY

COMPARE AND CONTRAST Explain to children what it means to *compare* and *contrast*. As you read about Satchel Paige and James Bell, encourage children to describe ways in which these men were the same and different. *(Possible responses: Both were great baseball players, both were African American. Paige was best-known for his pitching; Bell for his hitting.)* Use a Venn Diagram to help children organize their ideas.

VISUALIZE Have children picture their favorite teams or players and encourage children to describe what they see. Read the first page of the book and ask: Pretend you are a baseball fan many years ago. What does the picture in your mind look like when you read that African American players were not allowed in the major leagues?

ADDITIONAL SKILL INSTRUCTION

FACT AND OPINION Explain that a statement of a *fact* can be proved true or false and a statement of *opinion* expresses a belief or feeling. Read the last sentence on page 8 and help children determine whether it is a statement of fact or a statement of opinion. Say: Here it says that Cool Papa Bell entered the baseball Hall of Fame in 1974. Can this statement be proved true or false? What are some ways we could check?

Name _____

Compare and Contrast

In the book *Three of the Greats*, you learned about Satchel Paige and Josh Gibson. Compare and contrast these baseball players. Use the chart below to organize the facts. Write two facts for each player. Then, write one fact that they share.

Satchel Paige	Both	Josh Gibson

Name _____

Vocabulary

Choose a word from the box to complete the following story about baseball. Write the word on the line. The first one has been done for you.

Words to Know
bases   cheers   field   plate   sailed   threw

Playing baseball is a lot of fun, but I was nervous when

I got up to the _____ **plate** _____. The pitcher

_____ the ball. I hit it as hard as I could.

The ball _____ high through the air. It

landed far out in the _____. I ran around

the _____ as fast as I could. I heard loud

_____ from the crowd. I scored a home run!

Happy Birthday, America!

SUMMARY People in the United States celebrate July 4 as America's birthday. They celebrate with parades and barbecues. The Fourth of July is the day when America declared its independence from England in 1776. On the Fourth of July, people see symbols of America, such as the American flag and Uncle Sam.

LESSON VOCABULARY

America	birthday
flag	freedom
nicknames	stars
stripes	

INTRODUCE THE BOOK

INTRODUCE THE TITLE AND AUTHOR Point to the book title and author on the book cover, and read both out loud. Invite children to join in with you, if they like. Then speculate with children what this book might be about. Ask children if they think America has a birthday, and encourage children to share ideas for how people might celebrate such a birthday.

BUILD BACKGROUND Show children a large calendar page for July, and circle July 4. Say it for the class, and ask children what they think when they hear "the Fourth of July." Invite children to share their own experiences with this holiday. Conclude that the Fourth of July is America's birthday.

PREVIEW/TAKE A PICTURE WALK Invite children to take a picture walk through the book. Encourage them to call out ideas that the pictures evoke. You might ask children what conclusions they can make about this book. (This book will tell us about the United States; about the Fourth of July.)

READ THE BOOK

SET PURPOSE Work with children to set a purpose for reading Happy Birthday, America! Encourage children to consider questions they have about the book title and when, why, and how America celebrates a birthday. Suggest that children consider how they celebrate the Fourth of July or what this holiday means to them.

STRATEGY SUPPORT: MONITOR AND FIX UP Children may read words correctly but not understand exactly what they have read. Provide time for children to monitor their reading by questioning the information on each page. Tell children to reread to confirm understanding and to fix anything they did not understand.

COMPREHENSION QUESTIONS

PAGE 4 What information on this page is a fact, and what information is an opinion? (The Fourth of July is a holiday is a fact; calling it a great holiday is an opinion.)

PAGE 7 Is Uncle Sam a real person? (No, he is a symbol of the United States. People dress up to look like this symbol.)

PAGE 9 Why do people wave flags when they watch a parade on the Fourth of July? (Flags are a symbol of America. Waving a flag shows you understand what the Fourth of July means.)

PAGE 12 What should people remember about why we celebrate the Fourth of July? (We celebrate the Fourth of July to honor America's independence from England. Gaining this independence was not easy.)

REVISIT THE BOOK

READER RESPONSE

1. Opinion
2. Possible responses for web: symbol of America; Philadelphia; Independence Hall; made in 1752; cracked; remade two more times; last rang in 1846; still has a crack
3. Possible response: our flag's design is made up of stars and stripes.
4. Possible response: It explains that Uncle Sam is sometimes shown as a cartoon.

EXTEND UNDERSTANDING Share with children that the date July 4 is a symbol of America; it is a symbol of America's freedom and independence. Ask children to look through the book for other examples of American symbols, such as the U.S. Capitol building, the American flag, Uncle Sam, and the Liberty Bell. You might work with children to create a paper quilt of these American symbols and others they know.

RESPONSE OPTIONS

WRITING Invite children to think about ways to celebrate the Fourth of July. Encourage children to write a few sentences to tell about their ideas, drawing on personal experiences. You might suggest a sentence starter, such as: *On July 4, we _____.*

WORD WORK Write the words *freedom* and *independence* on the board and say them with the group. Ask children to explain what *freedom* or *independence* means to them. Prompt children to give examples of times when they feel free or independent by asking them to complete the sentence: *I feel free when I _____.*

SOCIAL STUDIES CONNECTION

Time For SOCIAL STUDIES

Help children research how their community celebrates the Fourth of July. Show children pamphlets or brochures from your community, view a community Web site, or invite a community member to talk to the class about the celebration. Encourage children to make posters that inform others about the community's July 4 festivities.

Skill Work

TEACH/REVIEW VOCABULARY

Write the word *birthday* on the board, and ask children to explain its meaning. Make sure children understand that a birthday is the day on which someone—or something—is born. Encourage children to explain how America could have a birthday. Talk about what it means to say that America was born.

ELL Point to the flag in your classroom, and say, *flag.* Have children repeat the word with you. Point to the stripes on the flag, then the stars on the flag, and say the word for each, again asking children to say each word with you. Encourage children to draw a picture of a flag, and label it *flag,* then to draw in stars and stripes, labeling them, too.

TARGET SKILL AND STRATEGY

FACT AND OPINION Remind children that an *opinion* is an idea or the way someone feels. Opinions are not right or wrong. A *fact,* however, can be right or wrong. Encourage children to consider the information in the book as fact or opinion. For example, on page 6: The flag is an important symbol. It is a fact that the flag is a symbol. The word *important* expresses an opinion.

MONITOR AND FIX UP Remind children that when they *monitor* their reading, they check to make sure they understand what they have read. As children read, encourage them to pause after each page and to think about what they've learned. If they feel they do not understand the main idea, encourage them to reread the text.

ADDITIONAL SKILL INSTRUCTION

AUTHOR'S PURPOSE Share with children that when authors decide to write, they have a reason, or a *purpose,* for what they choose to write about. Encourage students to think about why the author wrote this book. Read with them the text on page 12 to prompt ideas.

Name _____

Fact and Opinion

Each sentence below is a statement of opinion. **Rewrite** them so it is a statement of fact. The first one has been done for you.

1. **Opinion:** The American flag is a terrific symbol.
   Fact:

   ## The American flag is a symbol.

2. **Opinion:** The Fourth of July is the most important holiday.
   Fact:
   _____
   _____

3. **Opinion:** Uncle Sam is a funny American symbol.
   Fact:
   _____
   _____

4. **Opinion:** The Liberty Bell rang loudly on July 4, 1776.
   Fact:
   _____
   _____

5. **Opinion:** After a parade, some people should have a barbecue.
   Fact:
   _____
   _____

Name _____

Vocabulary

Read each word.

Draw a line to the picture that best shows the meaning of the word.

1. flag

a.

2. stripes

b.

3. America

c.

4. stars

d.

Read each sentence. Write a word from the box that best fits each sentence.

birthday   freedom   nicknames

5. The Stars and Stripes is one of the _____ for the American flag.

6. July 4 is America's _____ .

7. America gained its _____ from England many years ago.

Very Special Birthdays

SUMMARY In this book, children will learn some typical ways that the Chinese celebrate birthdays.

LESSON VOCABULARY

aunt	bank
basket	collects
favorite	present

INTRODUCE THE BOOK

INTRODUCE THE TITLE AND AUTHOR Discuss with children the title and author of *Very Special Birthdays*. Does the title and cover art make them want to read the book? Why or why not?

BUILD BACKGROUND Invite children to discuss ways in which their own families or cultures celebrate birthdays. Point out where China is on a classroom map. Ask if anybody knows any special ways that the Chinese culture might celebrate birthdays. Let children know that in the Chinese culture, different birthdays are celebrated in different ways, and that they will be learning more about that in the book.

PREVIEW/TAKE A PICTURE WALK Have children look through the book. Point out the first heading *Birthdays Are Special*, and then ask children to look for the other heads as they preview the book. Afterwards, ask them what they think they will learn in the book. Briefly introduce the idea that the book will be about Chinese birthday celebrations. How do they think the headings will help them understand what they are reading?

READ THE BOOK

SET PURPOSE Have children set a purpose for reading *Very Special Birthdays*. Remind children of what they learned when previewing the book. Let children's interest in birthdays and other cultures guide their purpose. They might want to find out what kind of presents children get, or what special food is served. They might also want to discover how the birthday celebrations are different from their own.

STRATEGY SUPPORT: SUMMARIZE Have children tell you what they think it means to summarize something. If necessary, review that to summarize something is to give the main, or most important, ideas in one's own words. Ask students to watch for main ideas as they read so they can summarize.

COMPREHENSION QUESTIONS

PAGE 5 Why are guests given red eggs at parties for new babies? *(Red means happiness; eggs mean new life.)*

PAGES 8–9 What is one way that the first birthday is different from other birthdays? *(Possible response: Baby chooses an object that shows what his or her future job might be.)*

PAGE 10 What kind of noodles are served at birthday celebrations. Why? *(Long noodles for a long life)*

PAGE 12 Why do you think the different foods are so important to Chinese birthday celebrations? *(Possible response: Each food has a different meaning, but they all are supposed to be signs of good things.)*

REVISIT THE BOOK

READER RESPONSE

1. Red is for happiness; money is fortune; the wrapped paper could mean good or happy fortune.
2. Use chart to summarize. One Month: lots of family; baby chooses object for future; Sixtieth: lots of family, sharing eggs, noodles, and peaches for long life
3. Possible responses: A picnic basket holds foods and has handles; a basketball is thrown into a basket or hoop.
4. Answers will vary.

EXTEND UNDERSTANDING Invite children to compare Chinese birthday celebrations with their own experiences of birthday celebrations. What is similar? What is different?

RESPONSE OPTIONS

WRITING Invite children to write invitations to the Chinese birthday celebrations of a newborn baby, a one-year-old baby; and a sixty-year-old person.

SOCIAL STUDIES CONNECTION

Time For SOCIAL STUDIES

Encourage children to find out more about Chinese celebrations. Afterwards, have children share information about the celebrations that interested them the most.

Skill Work

TEACH/REVIEW VOCABULARY

Pass out cards that have vocabulary words on them. Have children use their words in sentences that relate to the idea of birthdays or birthday parties.

ELL To help make sure children understand the vocabulary, invite them to go through the book and point to the pictures that best illustrate the words. (Page 6 shows a present, the woman on page 5 could be an aunt, etc.)

TARGET SKILL AND STRATEGY

DRAW CONCLUSIONS Remind children to use the pictures and what they already know about birthdays to help them figure out more about what they are reading. Ask: Why do some guests give a new baby clothes decorated with tigers? (They believe that tigers protect the baby, so if the baby wears the clothing with tigers on it, the baby will be protected.)

SUMMARIZE Discuss that to *summarize* something is to give the main, or most important, ideas in your own words. To do that, children should think about what the information or story is mostly about. In *Very Special Birthdays,* taking the time to summarize sections after they read them will help children better understand and remember what they are learning about Chinese birthdays and how each of them is different.

ADDITIONAL SKILL INSTRUCTION

COMPARE AND CONTRAST Review with children that to *compare* and *contrast* means to see how things are alike and how they are different. As children read, suggest they pay attention to how the one-month, one-year, and sixtieth birthday celebrations are the same, and how they are different.

Name_____

Draw Conclusions

Think about what you know about Chinese birthday celebrations after reading. Then answer the questions.

Write a few sentences that tell about what happened in the story.

1. Why do you think new babies get gifts with tigers on them?

_____

- -

_____

2. How do you know that birthdays are an important part of Chinese culture?

_____

- -

_____

_____

- -

_____

3. How do you know that eating special foods is an important part of Chinese birthday celebrations?

_____

- -

_____

_____

- -

_____

4-5. Which of the birthday celebrations do you think you would like the most? Why?

_____

- -

_____

_____

- -

_____

Name_____

Vocabulary

Choose the word from the box that best fits each sentence.
Each vocabulary word is used one time.

Words to Know
aunt   bank   basket   collects   favorite   present

_____
1. The _____ was filled with toys.

_____
2. A _____ is a safe place to keep money.

_____
3. My _____ gave me a birthday present.

_____
4. Red is my _____ color.

_____
5. My brother _____ the gifts and puts

them in a basket.

Write a word that means the same as the word *gift*.

_____
6. _____

Ranch Life

SUMMARY Eight-year-old Emma lives on a ranch in the American West, more than a hundred years ago. She helps her family do many tasks, both indoors and outdoors. One of the most thrilling aspects of ranch life for Emma is watching the cowboys as they handle the cattle. This realistic historical fiction gives readers a glimpse into ranch life, long ago.

LESSON VOCABULARY

campfire	cattle	cowboy
galloped	herd	railroad
trails		

INTRODUCE THE BOOK

INTRODUCE THE TITLE AND AUTHOR Present the book to the group, and have children read the book title and author name with you. Based on the book title, encourage children to predict what this book will be about. Ask: Who might the girl be on the cover? Record children's predictions to review after reading.

BUILD BACKGROUND Invite children to explain what they think living on a ranch might have been like. Ask: Which workers might you see on a ranch? Write the word *cowboy* on the board, and invite children to describe images and ideas that this word evokes. Then ask children what job cowboys (and cowgirls) do, and list their ideas.

PREVIEW Before they preview the pictures, ask children to share their impressions about what a ranch looks like. Ask: What scenery do you expect to see? What buildings? What animals? What clothing might the people wear? Have children then view the pictures to confirm and amend ideas.

READ THE BOOK

SET PURPOSE Point out to children that this book isn't titled *Cowboy Life*, but *Ranch Life*. As they read, encourage children to look for the ways in which cowboys fit into ranch life. Also suggest that children pay attention to how the main character of this story, Emma, feels about cowboys.

STRATEGY SUPPORT: GRAPHIC ORGANIZERS Suggest that children use a word web to record words or phrases that tell about what life is like on a ranch. In the center circle of the web, instruct them to write *Ranch Life*. Have them attach four outer circles in which to record additional ideas.

COMPREHENSION QUESTIONS

PAGE 4 What happened is that Emma planted seeds for pumpkins, corn, and cucumbers. When did it happen? *(After Papa turned over the soil in the garden.)*

PAGE 6 How is the task described here the same yet different for Emma and Mama? Write your ideas in a Venn Diagram. *(Mama: sews sheets and clothes; Both: they both sew; Emma: sews an apron for herself)*

PAGE 8 How does Emma feel about watching the cowboys? *(has fun watching them keep cattle from running away)*

PAGE 11 Why would cowboys no longer be needed if a railroad were built near the ranch? *(The train could take the cattle into town, replacing the cowboys.)*

REVISIT THE BOOK

READER RESPONSE

1. The cowboys would no longer be needed at the ranch because trains could take the cattle to town.
2. Possible responses: Outdoor Jobs: planting, bringing in water, fishing; Indoor Jobs: cooking, sewing, writing letters
3. cows; roundup, fireplace
4. Children's responses will vary. Encourage children to include details about ranch life that they read about in the book.

EXTEND UNDERSTANDING Have children study the pictures and think about the story. Ask: Does this story take place in the past or in the present? What details identify this story as being realistic and in the past? *(the clothing, the fact that the home has no running water or modern appliances, Emma writing with a quill and not a pen)* Share with children that recognizing the time period in which a story takes place extends their understanding.

RESPONSE OPTIONS

WRITING Remind children that Emma writes letters to people "back East." Invite children to imagine that they live on a ranch, and have them write a few sentences to tell someone what their life is like. You might share with children how to set up a letter to make their writing seem more authentic.

SOCIAL STUDIES CONNECTION

Time For SOCIAL STUDIES

Display a map of the United States. Recall that some of Emma's friends and family are "back East." Point to the East Coast of the United States. Then point to western states, such as Montana, Wyoming, and Texas, and explain that many states in the West have cattle ranches. You might also discuss that during Emma's time, telephones and computers had not yet been invented. The only way to communicate with people far away was to write letters. Speculate with children other things they might miss if they lived during Emma's time. Also encourage children to share what they would enjoy about living on a ranch, long ago.

Skill Work

TEACH/REVIEW VOCABULARY

Have children close their eyes, and tell them to listen as you say the vocabulary words. Encourage children to picture the words in their minds as you say them. Have children open their eyes, and invite them to share what they visualized as you said the words.

ELL Ahead of time, create simple picture cards for each vocabulary word. Label each picture with a vocabulary word. Present each card, one at a time. Point to the picture, then point to the word and say it aloud. Point to the picture again, and have students say the word with you. To check that children know the words, you might display the cards in random order. Say a word, and have children point to the correct card.

TARGET SKILL AND STRATEGY

CAUSE AND EFFECT Review with children that one event often causes another event to happen. As they read, challenge students to think about what happens, and about why it happened. For example, on page 4, Papa turned over the soil in the garden is what happened. It got warm is why it happened.

GRAPHIC ORGANIZERS Share with children that *graphic organizers* are useful tools. They help readers organize and view information in structured ways. Review some graphic organizers (Venn Diagrams, T-charts, word webs, flow charts, and time lines), drawing them on the board.

ADDITIONAL SKILL INSTRUCTION

REALISM AND FANTASY Invite children to talk about the difference between *realism* and *fantasy*. Confirm that *realism* involves characters, settings, and actions that could really happen; *fantasy* involves characters, settings, and actions that cannot happen in the real world. Ask: Do you think the book *Ranch Life* has mostly elements of realism or fantasy? Confirm that the story elements are real. Encourage children to explain why the elements are real and not elements of fantasy.

Name _____

Cause and Effect

The sentences on the left tell a **cause**.
The sentences on the right tell an **effect**.
Draw a line to match each cause with its effect.

Cause	**Effect**
I. Emma plants seeds.	**a.** Papa hired cowboys to bring his cattle together.
2. Emma's friends and family live far away.	**b.** Vegetables will soon grow.
3. The cattle must get to town.	**c.** The ranch might not need cowboys anymore.
4. A railroad might be built near the ranch.	**d.** Emma stays in touch with family and friends by writing letters.

5. Read the sentence below.
   CAUSE: It is hot and sunny today.
   Write a sentence to tell an effect.
   EFFECT:

_____

- -

_____

- -

_____

Name _____

Vocabulary

Look at each picture. Which word tells about it?
Circle the correct word for each picture.

1.

cattle   cowboy

2.

trails   railroad

3.

ranch   campfire

4.

cowboy   campfire

5.

trail   ranch

6.

galloped   herd

7. Use the word *galloped* in a sentence.

_____

_____

_____

_____

At the Powwow

SUMMARY A Native American boy attends a powwow ceremony with his family and learns about some of his tribe's traditions.

LESSON VOCABULARY

borrow	clattering
drum	jingle
silver	voice

INTRODUCE THE BOOK

INTRODUCE THE TITLE AND AUTHOR Discuss with children the title and author of *At the Powwow*. Do any of the children know what the word *powwow* means? Can they guess what it might mean from the picture on the cover of the book?

BUILD BACKGROUND If children do not know or weren't able to guess what a powwow is, tell them that it is a Native American celebration and they will be learning more about it in this book. Tell them that whole families participate in the powwows. Ask them if there are any celebrations that their family likes to attend.

PREVIEW/TAKE A PICTURE WALK Invite children to look at the pictures in the book. Ask them to tell you where most of the story takes place. What do they think might happen in this story? Why?

READ THE BOOK

SET PURPOSE Have children set a purpose for reading *At the Powwow*. Do they want to learn what happens at a powwow? Do they want to see if Ben will like being at a powwow?

STRATEGY SUPPORT: PRIOR KNOWLEDGE Tell students to think about what they already know about Native American culture and family celebrations. Discuss and display a KWL chart such as the one at the back of the book. Help them to fill in the first two columns. After reading, work together to fill in the last column. Then, ask children if they thought filling in the chart helped them better understand what they were reading.

COMPREHENSION QUESTIONS

PAGE 3 Do you think Ben has been to many powwows? Why or why not? (*He has not been to many powwows; He asks his grandmother to tell him about them.*)

PAGE 5 What do Ben's parents do to get ready for the powwow? (*put on special costumes*)

PAGE 11 How does Ben feel at the end of the powwow? (*happy that he got to spend a special day with his family*)

REVISIT THE BOOK

READER RESPONSE

1. Setting: powwow; Characters: Ben, Gram, Mom, Dad
2. Responses will vary.
3. Possible responses: rattling, banging, clanking
4. Possible response: Drums are important to Native Americans like our beating hearts are important to our bodies.

EXTEND UNDERSTANDING To help children understand Ben's character and his experiences at the powwow, invite them to pretend that they are Ben and have just returned from the powwow. Have children describe what they saw and heard, and how that made them feel. Guide them to make sure that their descriptions and feelings are based on both the text and the illustrations. Afterward, discuss whether or not role-playing Ben made it easier to understand his experience.

RESPONSE OPTIONS

VISUAL Have children draw pictures of a special celebration day they spent with their own families. Then, have them write a few sentences about what is happening in the picture.

SOCIAL STUDIES CONNECTION

Time For SOCIAL STUDIES

Provide books or Internet access for children to explore how different Native American groups celebrate powwows. Invite children to share information they've learned with each other.

Skill Work

TEACH/REVIEW VOCABULARY

Challenge children to use as many vocabulary words as possible in one sentence. Example: I would like to *borrow* your *silver drum*.

ELL Point out that *clattering* and *jingle* are both words that describe sounds. Use objects in the room to demonstrate clattering and jingling sounds.

TARGET SKILL AND STRATEGY

CHARACTER, SETTING, PLOT Review with children that *characters* are *who* are in the story and *setting* is *where* and *when* the story takes place. What happens in the story is the *plot*. Have children identify the main characters. *(Ben, Gram, Mom, Dad)* Remind children that just as there may be more than one character in a story, there may be more than one setting. Have children identify the setting at the beginning of the story. *(Ben's home)*

PRIOR KNOWLEDGE Review with children that thinking about what they already know, or *prior knowledge,* will help them to better understand what is happening in a story and what might happen next. Model text-to-self connections by reading page 3 aloud and then talking about it: "This page tells me that Ben is going to hear stories and songs and see dances at the powwow. I have been to celebrations like that. They were a lot of fun. In the picture, Ben looks happy to be hearing about the powwow. I bet Ben is going to have fun at the powwow." Invite children to share their own experiences of big celebrations.

ADDITIONAL SKILL INSTRUCTION

THEME After children have read the book, encourage them to think about the big idea of the story. Ask: What does this story tell you about people? What are the important ideas about family and tradition? How does this story remind you of something that happened in your family? Encourage students to think about how the story relates to them as readers.

Name_____

Character, Setting, Plot

Draw a picture of Ben at a powwow. Show how Ben feels.

1-2.

Write a few sentences that tell about what happened in the story.

3. Beginning: _____

4. Middle: _____

5. End: _____

Name_____

Vocabulary

Circle the word that best fits into each sentence. Then, write it on the line.

_____

1. Sally plays the _____.

drain   drum   dress

_____

2. My new ring is made out of _____.

slip   sling   silver

_____

3. Please don't talk in such a loud_____.

vest   choice   voice

_____

4. Can I _____ your pencil to write a letter?

borrow   bored   broom

Circle the words that describe a sound.

5. Jingle   Very   Clattering   Class   Clown   Jump

Story Prediction from Previewing

Title _____

Read the title and look at the pictures in the story.
What do you think a problem in the story might be?

I think a problem might be _____

_____

_____

After reading _____ ,
draw a picture of one of the problems in the story.

Story Prediction from Vocabulary

Title and Vocabulary Words

Read the title and the vocabulary words.
What do you think this story might be about?

I think this story might be about _____

_____

_____

After reading _____ ,
draw a picture that shows what the story is about.

KWL Chart

Topic _____

What We **K**now	What We **W**ant to Know	What We **L**earned

Vocabulary Frame

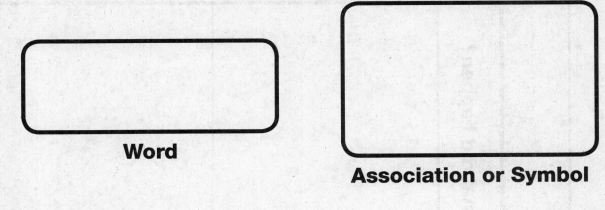

Word

Association or Symbol

Predicted definition: _____

_____

One good sentence:

_____

_____

_____

Verified definition: _____

_____

_____

Another good sentence:

_____

_____

_____

Story Predictions Chart

Title _____

What might happen?	What clues do I have?	What did happen?

Story Sequence A

Title _____

Beginning

Middle

End

Story Sequence B

Title	
Characters	**Setting**

Events 1. First	

2. Next	

3. Then	

4. Last	

© Pearson Education

Story Sequence C

Title

Characters

Problem

Events

_____

_____

_____

_____

_____

_____

_____

_____

Solution

Question the Author

Title _____

Author _____ **Page** _____

1. What does the author tell you?	
2. Why do you think the author tells you that?	
3. Does the author say it clearly?	
4. What would make it clearer?	
5. How would you say it instead?	

Story Comparison

Title A _____

_____

Characters

Setting

Events

Title B _____

_____

Characters

Setting

Events

Web

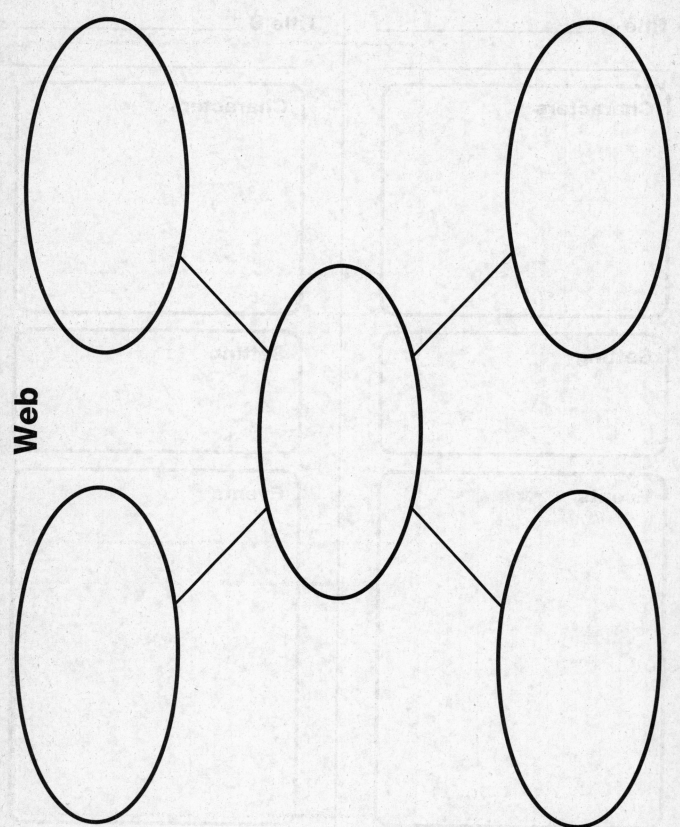

Main Idea

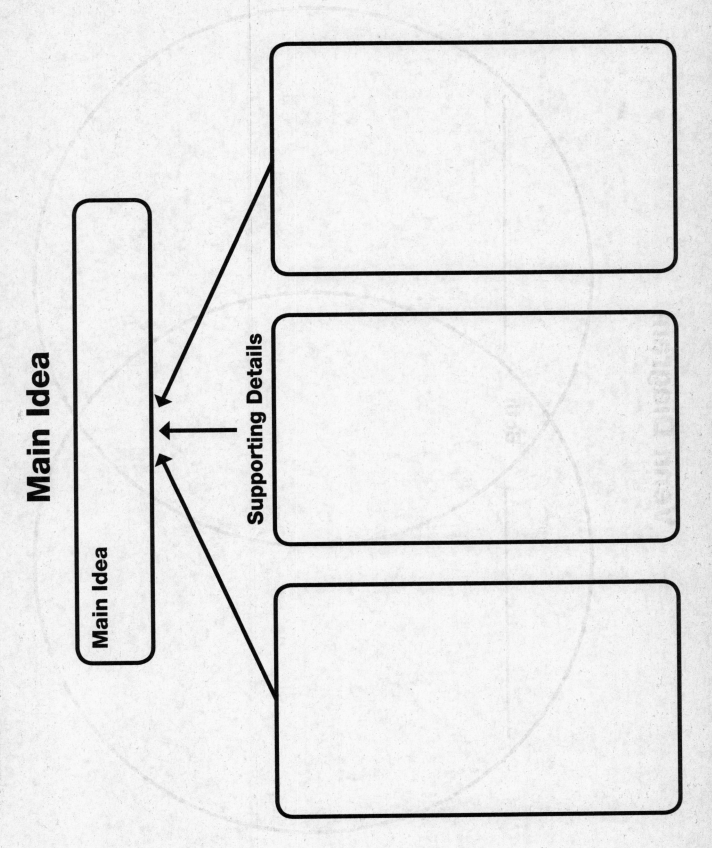

Main Idea

Supporting Details

Venn Diagram

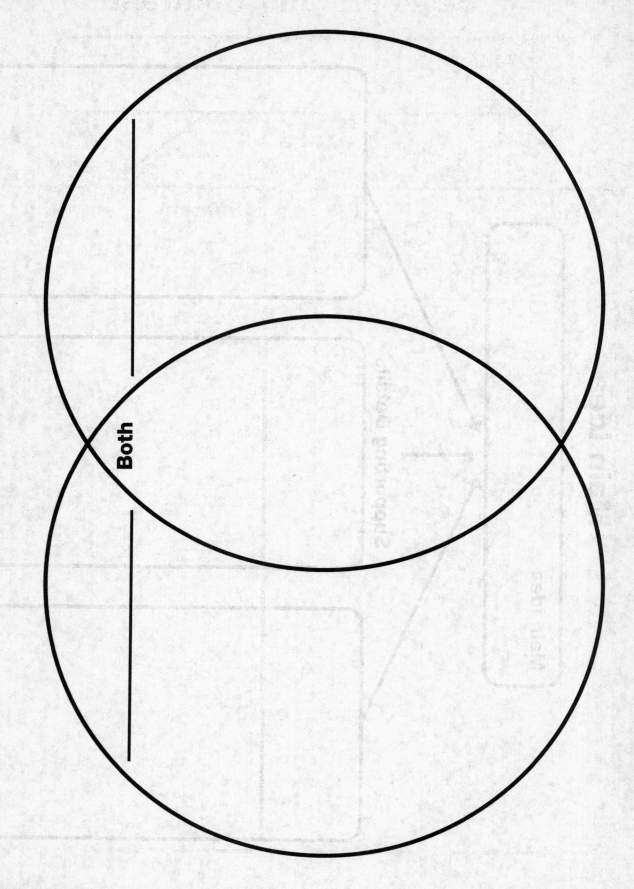

Both

Compare and Contrast

Topics

Alike

Different

Cause and Effect

Causes   **Effects**

Why did it happen?	What happened?
Why did it happen?	What happened?
Why did it happen?	What happened?

Problem and Solution

Problem

Attempts to Solve the Problem

Solution

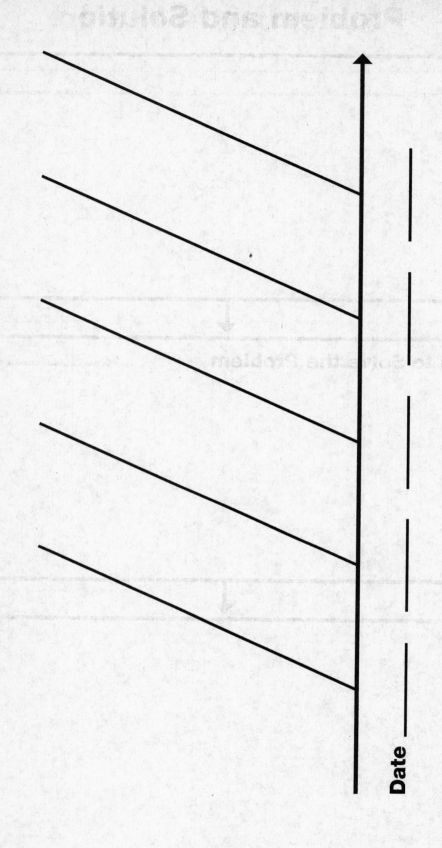

Time Line

Date

Steps in a Process

Process _____

┌───┐
│ **Step 1**   │
│   │
│   │
│   │
└───┘
                    ↓
┌───┐
│ **Step 2**   │
│   │
│   │
│   │
└───┘
                    ↓
┌───┐
│ **Step 3**   │
│   │
│   │
│   │
└───┘

Three-Column Chart

Four-Column Chart

Four-Column Graph

Title _____

Answer Key

Leveled Reader Practice Pages

City Mouse and Country Mouse p. 14

⟡ **CHARACTER AND SETTING**

Setting: city, bakery, sidewalk, club
1. a c e
2. b d e

City Mouse and Country Mouse

p. 15 Vocabulary
1. c
2. a
3. b
4. On my birthday I feel like someone special.
5. Each winter, we take a trip somewhere warm.

Being an Astronaut p. 18

⟡ **MAIN IDEA AND DETAILS**

Possible responses given.
Topic: where astronauts sleep
Main Idea: Astronauts sleep in different places.
Supporting Details: Some use sleeping bags. Some sleep in bunks.

Being an Astronaut p. 19 Vocabulary
1. b
2. c
3. d
4. a
5. world, machines, work

Pup Camps Out p. 22

⟡ **CHARACTER AND SETTING**
1. b
2. c
3. a
4. a
5. Possible response given: Pup likes to camp.

Pup Camps Out p. 23 Vocabulary
1. d
2. a
3. b
4. c
5. bear, couldn't, straight

Desert p. 26

⟡ **MAIN IDEA AND DETAILS**
1. desert
2. The desert can be hot and dry, but it has many plants and animals.
3. You can see and hear different animals. Many flowers and trees grow in the dry desert.

Desert p. 27 Vocabulary
1. a
2. e
3. e
4. w
5. w
6. f
7. Possible response given: The desert is full of animals.

Missing Fish p. 30

⟡ **REALISM AND FANTASY**
1. F
2. F
3. R
4. F
5. R

Missing Fish p. 31 Vocabulary
1. pieces
2. learn
3. though
4. together
5. often
6. gone
7. very
8. Possible response given: "I often take a bath on Tuesday."

Dogs to the Rescue p. 34

⟡ **SEQUENCE**

5
4
2
3
1

Dogs to the Rescue p. 35 Vocabulary
1. family-3
2. heard-1
3. listen-2
4. pull-1
5. once-1
6. break-1
7. Answers will vary but should reflect students' understanding of the word.

Let's Play Baseball! p. 38
◎ REALISM AND FANTASY
1. fantasy
2. realistic story
3. fantasy
4. realistic story
5. fantasy

Let's Play Baseball! p. 39 Vocabulary
1. b
2. a
3. f
4. c
5. e
6. d
7. g
8. i
9. j
10. h

Busy Beavers p. 42
◎ SEQUENCE
1. Beavers cut down trees with their teeth.
2. They cut off the branches.
3. They cut off the bark.
4. They carry the logs toward the stream.

Busy Beavers p. 43 Vocabulary
1. whole
2. toward
3. word
4. ago
5. enough
6. above
Important word: lodge

Dogs at Work p. 46
◎ AUTHOR'S PURPOSE
1. a
2. a
3. c
4. Answers will vary.

Dogs at Work p. 47 Vocabulary
1. c
2. f
3. e
4. d
5. a
6. b
7. Answers will vary.

Together for Thanksgiving p. 50
◎ DRAW CONCLUSIONS
1. a
2. b
3. a
4. Possible response given.
   Thanksgiving is a day for sharing.

Together for Thanksgiving p. 51 Vocabulary
1. sorry
2. door
3. Everybody
4. brought
5. promise
6. minute
7. behind
8. brought

The Science Fair p. 54
◎ AUTHOR'S PURPOSE
Possible response given.
1. to teach how to do something
2. The author explains how the class made a volcano.
3. to show excitement
4. The author tells the story of how the class won the science fair.

The Science Fair p. 55 Vocabulary
1. science
2. shoe
3. pretty
4. guess
5. village
6. won
7. watch

How Does Mail Work? p. 58

🔎 **DRAW CONCLUSIONS**

1. c
3. b
2. a
4. d
5. Possible response given: I will get my mail today.

How Does Mail Work? p. 59 Vocabulary

1. swer
5. ture
2. pany
6. ash
3. away
7. ool
4. ents
8. Pictures and sentences will vary.

Casting Nets p. 62

🔎 **CAUSE AND EFFECT**

1. c
3. a
2. d
4. b
5. Sentences will vary.

Casting Nets p. 63 Vocabulary

1. f
2. d
3. g
4. b
5. e
6. a
7. c
8. Possible response given: Whatever the noise was, it finally stopped.

Shy Ana p. 66

🔎 **THEME AND PLOT**

Possible responses given.
1. She was shy.
2. She helped her father shop.
3. She was not shy.
4. She stopped being shy.
5. People can get over their shyness.

Shy Ana p. 67 Vocabulary

1. many
2. alone
3. half
4. daughters
5. their
6. youngest
7. buy

An Orange Floats p. 70

🔎 **CAUSE AND EFFECT**

Possible responses given.
1. Clothes sink.
2. A scientist has a question.
3. A scientist does a test.
4. She uses fresh water.
5. She uses salt water.

An Orange Floats p. 71 Vocabulary

1. taught
2. clothes
3. hours
4. money
5. money, neighbor, only, question

The Butterfly Quilt p. 74

🔎 **COMPARE AND CONTRAST**

Quilts: can be used as blankets, can touch and see actual fabrics from old clothing, each is unique, can be very large.

Photographs: can't touch the fabrics or clothing, some are very old and only in black and white, copies can be made, usually small and easy to store in albums or boxes.

Both: help preserve memories, are visual reminders of the past, can be kept a long time.

The Butterfly Quilt p. 75 Vocabulary

1. trunks
2. wrapped
3. blankets
4. stuffing
5. quilt
6. unpacked
7. pretended

Grow a Tomato! p. 78

🔎 **FACT AND OPINION**

1. Statement of opinion
2. Statement of fact
3. Statement of fact
4. Statement of opinion
5. Statement of fact

Grow a Tomato! p. 79 Vocabulary
1. bumpy
2. roots
3. soil
4. vines
5. fruit
6. harvest
7. smooth

A Frog's Life p. 82
🔊 COMPARE AND CONTRAST
1. tadpole *circled with line* to underwater plants
2. frog *circled with line* to flies
3. Tadpole
4. Frog

A Frog's Life p. 83 Vocabulary
1. shed
2. skin
3. powerful
4. wonderful
5. a. crawls
   b. insects
   c. pond

A Big Change p. 86
🔊 PLOT AND THEME
1. Jen leaves the city
2. Jen goes fishing
3. Jen likes the country.
Possible responses.
4. Don't judge something until you try it. Change can be good.

A Big Change p. 87 Vocabulary
1. giant
2. block
3. strong
4. fair
5. Answers will vary.
6. Answers will vary.
7. Answers will vary.

Special Beach Day p. 90
🔊 FACT AND OPINION
1. fact
2. opinion
3. opinion
4. fact
5. opinion
6. opinion
7. fact
8. fact
9. opinion
10. fact

Special Beach Day p. 91 Vocabulary
1. branches
2. picnic
3. angry
4. clung
5. finger
6. pressing
7. special

Community Helpers p. 94
🔊 MAIN IDEA
Police officers help the people in a community live together in peace.

Community Helpers p. 95 Vocabulary
1. station
2. quickly
3. buildings
4. masks
5. tightly
6. roar
7. burning

Horse Rescue! p. 98
🔊 SEQUENCE
4, 2, 7, 3, 5, 1, 6

Horse Rescue! p. 99 Vocabulary
lightning, flashes, poured, pounded, storm, thunder, rolling. Look at the sky! Horses fly!

Sally and the Wild Puppy p. 102
🔊 THEME AND PLOT
1. end
3. beginning
4. middle

Sally and the Wild Puppy p. 103 Vocabulary
1. treat
2. chewing
3. wagged
4. practice
5. chased
6. grabbed
7. dripping

What an Adventure! p. 106
🔊 AUTHOR'S PURPOSE
1. a
2. c
3. c
4. b
5. a

What an Adventure! p. 107 Vocabulary

1. d
2. c
3. a
4. g
5. f
6. b
7. e

Grandpa's Sign p. 110

🔁 **REALISM AND FANTASY**

1. no
2. no
3. yes
4. yes
5. Possible response given.
   This is a realistic story because it could really happen.

Grandpa's Sign p. 111 Vocabulary

1. e
2. b
3. a
4. d
5. c
6. Possible response given.
   Andrew blamed himself for not telling about the sign.

Three of the Greats p. 114

🔁 **COMPARE AND CONTRAST**

Possible response given.
Satchel Paige: great pitcher, over 20 years
Both: African American
Josh Gibson: great hitter, 17 years

Three of the Greats p. 115 Vocabulary

threw, sailed, field, bases, cheers

Happy Birthday, America! p. 118

🔁 **FACT AND OPINION**

2. The Fourth of July is a holiday.
3. Uncle Sam is an American symbol.
4. The Liberty Bell rang on July 4, 1776.
5. After a parade, some people have a barbeque.

Happy Birthday, America! p. 119 Vocabulary

1. c
2. d
3. b
4. a
5 nicknames
6. birthday
7. freedom

Very Special Birthdays p. 122

🔁 **DRAW CONCLUSIONS**

Possible response given.

1. To protect the babies
2. There are very special ways of celebrating each birthday.
3. Different foods are served at all the different celebrations.
4–5. Responses will vary.

Very Special Birthdays p. 123 Vocabulary

1. basket
2. bank
3. aunt
4. favorite
5 collects
6. present

Ranch Life p. 126

🔁 **CAUSE AND EFFECT**

1. b
2. d
3. a
4. c
5. Possible response given.
   I will go to the beach.

Ranch Life p. 127 Vocabulary

1. cattle
2. railroad
3. campfire
4. cowboy
5. trail
6. herd
7. Sentences will vary.

At the Powwow p. 130

1–2. Pictures will vary.

Possible responses given.

3. Ben's family put on special clothes.
4. Everyone danced together.
5. Ben's family eats together.

At the Powwow p. 131 Vocabulary

1. drum
2. silver
3. voice
4. borrow
5. Jingle, Clattering